Self-Taught

Self-Taught

Moving From a Seat-Time Model to a Mastery-Learning Model

Chris Edwards

ROWMAN & LITTLEFIELD
Lanham • Boulder • New York • London

Published by Rowman & Littlefield

An imprint of The Rowman & Littlefield Publishing Group, Inc.
4501 Forbes Boulevard, Suite 200, Lanham, Maryland 20706
www.rowman.com

86-90 Paul Street, London EC2A 4NE, United Kingdom

Copyright © 2023 by Chris Edwards

All rights reserved. No part of this book may be reproduced in any form or by any electronic or mechanical means, including information storage and retrieval systems, without written permission from the publisher, except by a reviewer who may quote passages in a review.

British Library Cataloguing in Publication Information Available

Library of Congress Cataloging-in-Publication Data

Names: Edwards, Chris, 1977– author.
Title: Self-taught : moving from a seat-time model to a mastery-learning model / Chris Edwards.
Description: Lanham, Maryland : Rowman & Littlefield, [2023] | Includes bibliographical references. | Summary: "This is a comprehensive plan for education reform as school face teacher and staff shortages"— Provided by publisher.
Identifiers: LCCN 2022030902 (print) | LCCN 2022030903 (ebook) | ISBN 9781475868173 (Cloth : acid-free paper) | ISBN 9781475868180 (Paperback : acid-free paper) | ISBN 9781475868197 (epub)
Subjects: LCSH: MOOCs (Web-based instruction) | Distance education. | Web-based instruction. | Computer-assisted instruction. | Educational technology.
Classification: LCC LB1044.87 .E388 2023 (print) | LCC LB1044.87 (ebook) | DDC 371.35/8—dc23/eng/20220818
LC record available at https://lccn.loc.gov/2022030902
LC ebook record available at https://lccn.loc.gov/2022030903

♾️ The paper used in this publication meets the minimum requirements of American National Standard for Information Sciences—Permanence of Paper for Printed Library Materials, ANSI/NISO Z39.48-1992.

For students, teachers, and parents. You deserve better.

Contents

Acknowledgments		ix
Introduction		xi
1	The Civilization Conversation	1
2	The Brain and Education	13
3	The Seat-Time Model	27
4	The Seat-Time Model and Society	43
5	The Mastery-Learning Model	65
6	Why Education Is Sequestered From Economic Trends and Innovation and How to Change This	75
7	Workforce Development	95
Conclusion: How Do We Do This?		105
Bibliography		109
About the Author		113

Acknowledgments

As always, thank you to my editors Tom Koerner, Carlie Wall, and Kira Hall. Also, thank you to Michael Shermer at *Skeptic* magazine. Sanjay Sarma and the Open Learning Department at the Massachusetts Institute of Technology deserve a sincere appreciation for their discussions and amazing work. The Scientech Foundation of Indianapolis deserves thanks for their financial support for educational reform projects and so does the Education Department at Ball State University for working with me on programs that have had a positive impact on teachers and students.

Introduction

What would *you* do if you needed to learn something?

This should be the core question of education. Every stakeholder in public education, students, parents, teachers, doctoral thesis advisors, business leaders, and politicians should ask themselves this one question anytime a discussion on educational reform begins. It is a simple question, but one with the potential to overhaul the entire educational component of society. Here is why.

Imagine for a moment that you want to learn where all 196 countries (generously defined) are on a map. Would you

A. Try to learn the whereabouts of these countries while simultaneously trying to learn from four to six other topics over the course of a day, all while being physically constrained in a room with dozens of other students and kept on a schedule of movement that is stricter than what prisoners endure? (High school model)
B. Pay several hundred dollars, or more, and travel to a college campus where the content will be delivered to you via a series of lectures but only at specific times? (The collegiate model)
C. Go to the library and check out an atlas, and sit and study it? (Old school autodidact's model)
D. Download "World Map Quiz" to your phone and play it at the three different levels of difficulty? (Modern self-taught model)

Most people would choose option "D" because this is the cheapest and most accessible option in terms of time and cost. World Map Quiz can be downloaded for free on a cell phone and played during any moment of downtime throughout the day. If one assumes that most people purchase a cell phone for purposes other than specifically playing World Map Quiz, then the cost of the app is negligible. An additional bonus is that world maps are immediately accessible on Google Images and one can find news and information, the kind that helps create neuronal connections between a historical narrative and a place (once you find out that Argentina is named after silver, Ag, on the periodic table, you will no longer have trouble finding it on a map) in the human brain.

While Option C is also cheap and potentially effective, atlases can be large and cumbersome, and books have a tendency to remain unopened as busy people wait for mythical free time. Virtually no one, of their own volition, would choose to learn with options A or B unless coerced to do so by a program that required the completion of a course for the purpose of gaining a credential. The credentials are, inexplicably, based not upon actual demonstration of one's mastery of geography, but based upon whether or not a student actually spent enough hours in a class where mastery of geography was taught.

The great irony in scenario A is that a teacher who wanted her students to master geography by playing World Map Quiz would be precluded from doing so by the entire educational structure around her. A geography teacher can't say "download this app and play the game until you know where the countries are" to students for the same reason that an English teacher cannot say "spend a lot of time reading books you enjoy," to students: it is too obvious and easy, and the process cannot be easily entered into a grade book or made to fit with a seat-time model. Parents would demand to know what "grade" their children have; administrators would want to see detailed lesson plans and evidence that the teacher is working.

Someone should try this experiment: Divide 20 students in half. Put 10 of them in a high school or college geography course for one semester and put the other 10 in a separate room where they will play World Map Quiz for the same amount of time. Who do you think will have a greater mastery of geography at the end?

Keep asking my simple question of "what would you do if you needed to learn something?" and the entire absurdity of the educational structure becomes apparent. What if you wanted to learn about the life and works of Jane Austen? You could start by going to the library and getting her books for free. If you found the novels hard to follow, a Google search will take you to any number of sites with plot summaries and commentary. If you wanted a deeper "collegiate" experience, for about 15 or 20 dollars a month subscribe to Wondrium (formerly The Great Courses) and listen to Dr. Devoney Looser, an Austen expert, lecture about the work and life of Austen (as well as gaining access to thousands of hours of other high-level content).

In such a self-directed program, you could both enjoy the reading of Austen while gaining a deeper knowledge of the scholarship around her life and work. You can read as much or as little of Austen's writing as you like, and extend your knowledge as far as your interest goes. Even better, you can listen to or watch Dr. Looser's lectures while you exercise or do the dishes; you can pause your study if something else interests you or if your work or life schedule interrupts.

However, if you want a credential for learning about Jane Austen, none of this will be true. You will be required to read the books on a specific timeline regardless of how much interest you have; the scholarly content will be delivered to you only through a live lecture, in the same way it was delivered in the medieval university system, and you will be graded only on the amount of learning you were able to absorb within a specific time frame. A 20-year-old who leaves a course with a middling knowledge of Jane Austen will forever be a "C" student in the topic, regardless of whether he decides to pick up the subject again at a later time and then becomes a master of the content.

And for this less effective and less malleable educational option, a student will be charged up to one hundred times more in price.

Keep asking yourself this fundamental question of "what would I do if I needed to learn something?" and you will find the boundaries of self-education. While you can learn a master's degree worth of mathematics with nothing but a workbook and YouTube, there will come a point at the highest levels of thought when a mathematician will need a small number of experts to guide her study and review her work.

A would-be brain surgeon can gain a basic understanding of human anatomy and a thorough understanding of neuroscience from books and free sources (any one of us can watch the lectures and read the papers of the best professors for nothing) but the actual practice of neurosurgery clearly needs the guidance of experts and a hands-on practicum. Our essential question, then, will leave graduate school programs intact.

However, the more you ask yourself "what would I do if I needed to learn something?" the more you will see how many aspects of education are expensive and unnecessary. There will never be a time when you will need a principal or assistant principal. You will not need an athletic director and, nowhere in your autodidactic experience will you find yourself unable to proceed in the study of art history or the learning of Newton's Second Law unless you are surrounded by young people doing impressive things with inflatable balls. You can learn content in any subject without once needing to go to prom.

During the great pandemic shutdown of 2020, parents found out a lot of things about their schools. The physical building of the elementary school is almost indispensable. Parents need to work and kids need to be in a safe place during the day; but students learning over Zoom or other platforms found that they could get that kind of education more effectively on free or very cheap online platforms. Why did "Zoom University" cost so much, when the same information was available for nothing elsewhere? A student who found her tenured professors at Random-State University uninspiring could listen to her psychology professor over Zoom, or spend the same time watching Stanford's Robert Sapolsky on YouTube, so why is the better content free?

Many parents, nationwide, had the experience of finding from an online gradebook that their child was doing poorly in a class, only to watch the grade rise when the child turned in a few missing assignments. What did the rise in the grade reflect? What skill was mastered that justifies the corresponding rise in the grade? The educational system is only tangentially connected to the teaching of content and skills. When the pandemic forced the educational structure to be solely focused on content-based curriculum, the results were unimpressive.

Before beginning with the first chapter, a few biographical facts about my own educational experience and professional life are relevant here. Much of my interest in mastery-learning models comes from an experience late in my life as a college student. After graduating high school, I worked in a variety of manual labor jobs; in the two years after high school I worked as a farm hand, landscaper, drywall-hanger, and pusher of boxes at FedEx, before taking a job as a factory machinist and member of the United Auto Workers. I was able to take a few leaves of absence to attend school full time but found myself behind in my credit hours after making a transfer to the School of Education. That was when I discovered the university's distance-learning program.

Although the internet existed at that time; its function had not yet really expanded into education and so the correspondence work had to be done through the postal service. Despite being warned that "no one ever finishes these classes" I took 18 credit hours (6 courses) worth of them which was the maximum allowed. Working the night shift allowed me to finish my machining work without being pestered by management, and this allowed time for me to also work on the correspondence course. Each class required hundreds of pages of reading and about 50 pages of writing; the extra workload was no doubt an attempt to deter students from taking these classes.

But the experience was liberating for me. I did not have to sit in a circle. I did not have to listen to a professor talk about her own life and experiences. I did not have to learn for an hour and a half, wait several days, and then learn again for another hour and a half. Wearing dirty work clothes and sitting, after midnight, at a draughting desk in a dimly lit factory, I finally received a genuine education and continued to find educational programs that would allow me a greater level of autonomy to be largely self-taught.

I am both an educational researcher, having worked as the principal investigator in state-funded research projects, and a public-school teacher with two decades of experience. This allows me to see the educational structure from both the inside and the outside, to understand the broad problems with the educational structure as a researcher, and to directly see the impact of institutional policies on the classroom itself. Both perspectives lead me to the following conclusion: the American educational structure is about to face a collapse. This will not be a total collapse, but a partial structural fall that will weaken even the supports left standing.

Students of history, like myself, know better than to make absolute predictions about the future but a series of trends, to be outlined in the following chapters, would seem to make it extremely unlikely that the educational structure can continue, as is, for very much longer. Teaching has become unsustainably hard to do, and this has not only contributed to a potentially catastrophic teacher shortage but has also made it more likely that students will have a less-than-effective teacher. A nefarious connection between community property values and the local school district, particularly in affluent suburban regions, feeds an entire "public-school-to-college" system that is ruinously expensive and scandalously inefficient.

Secondary education cannot be fixed. Conservative attempts at educational reform, for reasons to be detailed, have made the situation worse. Schools are designed around a feudal structure, with money from local, state, and federal sources being given to local districts and spent at a local level. Each district decides how much to spend on teacher salaries, paraprofessionals, administrative packages, sports stadiums, transportations, etc.

The United States contains nearly 14,000 different public school districts (https://www.guide2research.com/research/american-school-statistics #:~:text=In%20the%20U.S.%2C%20school%20districts,home%20 to%2016%2C800%20school%20districts). This prohibits any large-scale reform effort because any plan to change education would have to be implemented in 14,000 different ways, cutting through bureaucracies and surviving massive rates of teacher turnover. Reform will not happen. There are multiple ways in which this system can collapse and that increases the possibility of it occurring.

As of 2017, the United States had 3.6 million teachers (https://admissionsly .com/how-many-teachers-are-there/#:~:text=Some%20teacher%20 statistics%3A%20as%20of,million%20being%20in%20private%20schools), almost a 1:1 ratio with the entire state of Connecticut, and about one out of one-hundred Americans are in education. For a top-down reform model to be successful in actual classrooms it would need to be attractive to this large population. In a system where educational tax dollars are syphoned off for bureaucratic salaries, sports stadiums, and nonsensical professional development schemes, it is unlikely that a new model will ever be developed that truly sustains and develops highly effective teachers.

If the educational system cannot be reformed, and that argument will be made in subsequent chapters, then it must be circumvented through the implementation of a new and more effective Mastery-Learning Model (MLM) of education.

My education as a researcher and my experience as a teacher are in secondary and higher education, which roughly corresponds with grades 7–12. Although some of the ideas presented here will involve recommendations for changes in grades K–6, much of what happens at that level falls outside the boundaries of my expertise. From what I have studied, however, the general conjecture should be that educators at the secondary level have a lot to learn from our elementary colleagues, but there is no versa after the vice.

To explain what I mean, I will pose a question to every secondary educator. If students are generally happier, as research indicates, at the elementary levels, then why do we ever stop celebrating birthdays, putting kids in cohorts, letting them spend the day with a smaller number of teachers, decorating rooms for Halloween, and having recess?

When we stop doing the things that make us happy, it should not surprise us that we become sadder.

The forthcoming chapters will begin with a discussion on the nature of civilization itself. The hierarchical structure of modern education, so destructive to learning, is connected to a specific narrative about the nature of civilization. That narrative is being rethought and the concept of decentralized structures, of an alternative pathway into and through civilization itself, can now exist. Educational researchers and authors too often act as if educational structures exist as a separate compartment to civilization, and this blinds educators to understanding that the feudal and hierarchical structure that is inherent in all schools is part of a particular narrative about human civilization.

Then, the narrative will turn toward intelligence, brain structure, and its connection (or lack thereof) to educational practices and materials. The second chapter will feature an analysis of the structural deficits in both K–12 and undergraduate education, and this will include a particular emphasis on the cost of undergraduate education and why it cannot continue to defy economic models. The third chapter will include a vision for a post-pandemic educational structure that moves away from a Seat-Time Model and toward a Mastery-Learning Model. This will also include a discussion of current positive trends in higher education and an argument for a cheap and comprehensive educational future.

The key thesis that will be presented in the following pages is this: Public education, probably from levels 7 through the collegiate experience, needs to move from a Seat-Time Model to an MLM. This shift will do the following:

A. Allow education to be delivered to students at all times and in more comfortable and less restrictive environments. (And have more free time and more sleep!)
B. Lessen the unsustainable levels of pressure that are now put on teachers.
C. Break up the nefarious relationship between school districts and property values.
D. Disrupt the "suburbs-to-campus" structure that has become unsustainably expensive for the families who participate and alienating for students who choose not to.
E. Allow people to work and begin adulthood while becoming educated. Also, allow people to enter into higher education at various points in their life, thus lessening the pressure on early levels of academic achievement.
F. End the concept of grades and replace it with a concept of mastery.
G. Provide a vastly greater level of equity by delivering to levels of education to students of all backgrounds.
H. Break up a costly and damaging educational bureaucracy.

Careful readers will notice a seeming contradiction in this Introduction. I have asserted that the American educational structure is too big and cumbersome, too feudal in its construction, to be reformed. Yet, there is clearly a vision for reform stated here. The educational bureaucracy cannot change; no individual in a feudal system has the power to change more than a specific fiefdom. What can happen is this: the creation of laws that would allow for students to attain degrees and credentials by showcasing their mastery of skills, partially through testing or through other means. Change must come from outside of the educational structure and must be implemented around existing bureaucratic institutions.

With that simple change, it will be possible for students to attain their education in a variety of ways. This will naturally facilitate a change in how the public views their schools and shift the conception of a teacher.

Again, education need not be complicated. When confronted with a new concept or plan, simply ask yourself "what would I do if I needed to learn something?"

Before embarking on the first chapter, several points need to be made. First, the title "self-taught" does not indicate that students should be left on their own to figure out their education. The major implication of the phrase should be that to be self-taught means to be *self-motivated* as opposed to passively reliant on educational institutions that may or may not be effective at actually teaching students. The entire educational structure discourages self-motivation by creating the appearance that it is the duty of schools, rather than of the learner, to become educated.

Second, my inspiration for writing generally flows from my reading. Because of this, I prefer to include excerpts from other books when appropriate instead of using footnotes. This method prevents me from engaging in the mild authorial sin of patchwriting and also will hopefully draw attention to some good books and papers written by other authors.

Third, Dr. Sanjay Sarma is the head of Open Educational Resources at MIT and he and his team developed the concept of the open MicroMasters program. Much more will be written about this later, but the MicroMasters differs from other online schools because it is very cheap, and it is open to anyone who wants to take it (being a master's degree, a bachelor's is a prerequisite). Purdue Global offers online master's degrees of high quality, but they reject 99% of applicants and this means that Purdue is still investing their reputation in the exclusivity of entrance rather than in the mastery of skills.

In June of 2021, Harvard and MIT joined together with the online education platform edX. This was a $800 million deal. Two of the top universities in the world, Harvard and MIT, are planning to create Massive Open Online Courses (MOOCs) at the graduate level to provide cheap and challenging education to anyone across the globe who can master the skills and content in their respective fields.

I have reviewed the criticisms of MOOCs carefully, not for the purpose of refuting the argument but for finding ways to meaningfully address those criticisms with a new vision. Mastery Learning can be implemented in public schools, and it can be the core of post-secondary education. Clearly, parents need to be able to send their children to school during the day so that parents can work. Also, schools perform essential functions for the differently abled and can also be places of stability. Those functions can certainly continue and will likely be improved, by a Mastery-Learning Model.

In addition, teachers will be more important than ever in this new vision. MOOCs can be incredibly powerful educational tools, but teachers will need to give face-to-face contact to help students. Equally as important, an MOOC should have several gaps built into it so that teachers can fill those gaps with curricula that are tailored to the needs of the local community. This means that teachers' professional development should involve getting teachers out into their communities so that they can learn about what is happening, then create curricula based on that learning and implement them in their own classrooms. Instead of teachers being pawns controlled by a medieval hierarchy, which is what we have now, they will be connected to their communities and will shape the boundaries of their field just like professionals in the sciences do.

At all times, in writing this book, I tried to synthesize my experiences as a teacher and researcher. The first chapter, and a few of the sections of this book, have been published in the science and philosophy journal *Skeptic*. *Skeptic*'s editorial board includes some of the top intellectuals in the fields of history, science, and mathematics. There is academic value in having some aspects of an argument peer-reviewed by experts and then published in part, before being synthesized into a longer argument through a book.

Educators have not discovered a way to capture the enormous intellectual force that comes from self-teaching. In my first book on education, *Teaching Genius: Redefining Education With Lessons From Science and Philosophy* (2012), I noted that "genius" is not some mysterious characteristic. It only appears to be that way because a work of genius, by definition, must be novel and therefore will not usually occur just through the mastery of an established curriculum. The educational structure does not facilitate cross-curricular thinking, nor is there much room for the kind of bottom-up (even anarchic) approach to mastering knowledge that a work of genius requires.

I have often wondered why my self-education, which is driven by wandering through libraries and bookstores and shaped by a desire to make the classroom experience for my students as meaningful as possible, has always been so much more satisfying than the expensive educational structures, often simultaneously too rigid and too loose, that I have been through. It's not clear to me why the educational structure is almost never the answer when I ask myself "what would I do if I needed to learn something?"

Is it clear to you? If not, then let us change.

Chapter 1

The Civilization Conversation

A long time ago, in a continent far, far away . . .

Hunter-gatherers spread out from Africa and settled the world; their linguistic and social abilities, along with their ability to throw weapons, and a general ability to adapt to new environments, allowed for humans to survive and thrive in just about every ecological region on the planet. Then, climate change forced some of those hunter-gatherer tribes to look for stable food supplies, and in the areas where the geography was favorable, this led to the cultivation of cereal crops and the domestication of animals. By proxy, animals gave humans diseases, and this began a process of disease evolution with the human immune system.

Farming led to food surpluses, and this allowed for some people in society to specialize in activities like fighting wars, priesting, and working to solve the problems that civilization itself created. Those problems, like how to map out farms, create irrigation canals, deal with sewage, or build monumental architecture, forced humans to think in novel ways and create writing and mathematics. The human brain is pre-adapted for civilization in the same way that feathers which were used for warmth are pre-adapted for flying, and the new challenges of civilization rewired the hunter-gatherer brain.

This process first began in various regions, and in isolation, until technology made it possible for civilizations to move, trade, fight, and synthesize. The supercontinent of Eurasia was more suitable to this process than was the supercontinent of the Americas, and so after 1492, Eurasian civilization more or less transported itself across the Atlantic into the New World. This process brought with it the horrors of disease and enslavement, but gradually scientific and intellectual progress has turned civilization itself into something that creates progress in the human condition.

Even if we recognize the drawbacks that come from having hunter-gatherers live in a civilization, the general outlook is positive. Hierarchy, capitalism, and inequality must have survived this process for a reason; hierarchical control and bureaucratic rule are necessary to control large population densities and are on the right-hand side of the equal (unequal?) sign that comes from this established "civilization equation."

This narrative, which in rough outline approximates the state of the history of civilization as we enter the third decade of the 21st century, is the focus of David Graeber and David Wengrow's 2021 book *The Dawn of Everything: A New History of Humanity*.[1] It promises to upend the conversation about civilization and its origins.

A NEW DAWN

The Dawn of Everything overtly backs a particular political thesis. David Graeber (1961–2020) developed his skills for analyzing ancient cultures as an anthropologist and then used these skills to provide a perspective on Western industrial life. Graeber was a politically active anarchist (he was one of the leaders of the Occupy Wall Street movement), meaning that he did not believe in hierarchical control and saw direct similarities between bureaucrats in Soviet society and the purposeless jobs that existed in corporations. His books on bureaucracy and "bullshit jobs" provide a theoretical construct for understanding much about capitalist economies.[2] This central argument—that our current political and economic structure is the inevitable result of deterministic forces that are largely outside the control of human actors—is the primary target of *The Dawn of Everything*.

Hierarchical systems, the old argument goes, be they capitalist, communist, or fascist, must come with civilization because no system that is decentralized, anarchic, and egalitarian could ever control a massive population of former hunter-gatherers trying to live together in societies with heavy population densities. To Graeber and Wengrow, such an assertion provides a false theoretical justification for modern society, but it also creates a confirmation bias among anthropologists who study ancient civilizations. It is hard to see anarchy in ancient bones and settlements if one is not looking for it. Conversely, it becomes too easy to see social stratification if one is looking for that instead. The authors write:

> This book is an attempt to tell another, more hopeful and more interesting story; one which, at the same time, takes better account of what the last few decades of research have taught us. Partly, this is a matter of bringing together evidence that has accumulated in archaeology, anthropology, and kindred disciplines; evidence that points towards a completely new account of how human societies developed over roughly the last 30,000 years. Almost all of this research goes against the familiar narrative . . .

> To give just a sense of how different the emerging picture is: it is clear now that human societies before the advent of farming were not confined to small, egalitarian bands. On the contrary, the world of hunter-gatherers as it existed before the coming of agriculture was one of bold social experiments, resembling a carnival parade of political forms, far more than it does the drab abstractions of evolutionary theory. Agriculture, in turn, did not mean the inception of private property, nor did it mark an irreversible step toward inequality. In fact, many of the first farming communities were relatively free of ranks and hierarchies. And far from setting class differences in stone, a surprising number of the world's earlier cities were organized on robustly egalitarian lines, with no need for authoritarian rulers, ambitious warrior-politicians, or even bossy administrators. (p. 4)

The authors build upon this concept to do something unusual for a book of anthropology: they refer to the general synthesis of civilization conversation as the "Hobbesian model" and posit that "Rousseau's story about how humankind descended into inequality from an original state of egalitarian innocence seems more optimistic (at least there was somewhere better to fall from), but nowadays it's mostly deployed to convince us that while the system we live under might be unjust, the most we can realistically aim for is a bit of modest tinkering" (p. 6).

Undercutting the Hobbesian model is a way of undercutting a justification for the current hierarchical capitalist system. This is a system where democratic political idealism is a distraction from the fact that most of us suffer while laboring endlessly for corporate hierarchical structures that are as oppressive to human dignity as one-party states. The authors attack the concept of "inequality" as an oppressive abstraction that cannot be, like a state over an economic system, overthrown or changed. Therefore, to ask (as Jared Diamond did in *Guns, Germs, and Steel*[3]) what are the roots of inequality, or to assert (as Steven Pinker does in *The Better Angels of Our Nature*[4]) that inequality is not so bad if the have-nots of today have much more than the haves of the past, is to defend a system that oppresses the human spirit.

Francis Fukuyama, whose two-volume work on the development of civilization—*The Origins of Political Order* (2011) and *Political Order and Political Decay* (2014)[5]—reflects a conservative think-tank fascination with bureaucracy, Graeber and Wengrow suggest, is just as much to blame (or credit) as Diamond is for perpetuating the myth of inevitability. After humans stopped roaming around, "Hierarchies began to emerge. There was no point in resisting, since hierarchy—according to Diamond and Fukuyama—is inevitable once humans adopt large, complex forms of organization" (p. 10).

There is much in *The Dawn of Everything* that is typical of the "we-were-better-off-before-civilization" genre. For example, the authors quote from a famous letter written by Benjamin Franklin about how whites who were captured by Indians and lived in native society for a while were unable to return to the stultifying civilization of the whites. There is also a criticism of modern anthropologists who see all movement of objects from region to region as evidence of trade networks, rather than as evidence of quirkier aspects of human behavior like long-distance vision quests for items or gambling societies among the women.

In the Graeber-Wengrow narrative, the story after 1492 is less one of western conquest of the Americas followed by European Enlightenment, and more one about how conversations with natives led to a synthesis of ideas. Here is how the authors described it in one of the most interesting passages in the book:

> If we ask, not "what are the origins of social inequality?" but "what are the origins of the question about the origins of social inequality?" (in other words, how did it come about that, in 1754, the Academie de Dijon would think this an appropriate question to ask?), then we are immediately confronted with a long history of Europeans arguing with one another about the nature of faraway societies: in this case, particularly in the Eastern Woodlands of North America. What's more, a lot of those conversations make reference to arguments that took place between Europeans and indigenous Americans about the nature of freedom, equality or for that matter rationality and revealed religion indeed, most of the themes that would later become central to Enlightenment political thought. (p. 30)

There are some profound consequences that come from asking "what are the origins of the question about the origins of social inequality?" The notion being that historical narratives are shaped by the questions and concerns of historians, and those questions and concerns might be arbitrary. Asking different questions can lead to entirely different forms of history, and therefore, different conceptions of the present.

Of course, anthropology and archaeology are supposed to be sciences, not just a bunch of philosophers staring at bones and pieces of settlements and spitballing speculations about human nature. The point Graeber and Wengrow make is that too many scientists misread the evidence because they are looking for evidence of inequality to answer the question of "why inequality?"

> Evidence of Institutional inequality in Ice Age societies, whether grand burials or monumental buildings, is sporadic. Richly costumed burials appear centuries, and often hundreds of miles, apart. Even if we put this down to the patchiness of the evidence, we still have to ask why the evidence is so patchy in the first place: after all, if any of these Ice Age "princes" had behaved like, say, Bronze Age (let alone Renaissance Italian) princes, we'd also be finding all the usual trappings of centralized power: fortifications, storehouses, palaces. Instead, over tens of thousands of years, we see monuments and magnificent burials,

but little else to indicate the growth of ranked societies, let alone anything remotely resembling "states." To understand why the early record of human social life is patterned in this strange, staccato fashion, we first have to do away with some lingering preconceptions about "primitive" mentalities. (p. 92)

What follows from such a statement is a vast and assorted array of evidence about how the assumptions that modern anthropologists and archaeologists, citizens of hierarchical and unequal states, simply fail to be supported by the evidence. Hierarchical organizations with private property are not inevitable results of settled farming, but anomalies. The catch is that once societies start moving in a hierarchical direction, they "get stuck" on that path and can't retreat from it. Take the case of the Calusa, a "non-agricultural people who inhabited the west coast of Florida, from Tampa Bay to the Keys" (p. 150). The Calusa, encountered by Ponce de Leon in 1513, skipped the agricultural stage and went straight to a centralized kingdom with built-in inequality.

By all accounts, then, the Calusa had indeed "got stuck" in a single economic and political mode that allowed extreme forms of inequality to emerge. But they did so without ever planting a single seed or tethering a single animal. Confronted with such cases, adherents of the view that agriculture was a necessary foundation for durable inequalities have two options: ignore them, or claim they represent some kind of insignificant anomaly. (p. 152)

Of course, a book that seeks to discuss and dismiss notions of inequality will by necessity have to address slavery, but the authors note how difficult the concept is to define and find when studying ancient societies. Slaves tended to be war captives, often women, and they "were an anomaly: people who were neither killed nor adopted, but who hovered somewhere in between; abruptly and violently suspended in the midpoint of a process that should normally lead from prey to pet to family" (p. 191).

To the author's credit, they don't pick through evidence that only supports their claims to equality. They note that "in any true Northwest Coast settlement hereditary slaves might have constituted up to a quarter of the population. These figures are striking . . . they rival the demographic balance in the colonial South at the height of the cotton boom . . ." (p. 199). Such passages indicate that the authors' real intent is to note that ancient societies are just too varied to draw any conclusion about notions of inequality in society. The authors seem to imply that if you want evidence for a theory, the archaeological record will supply it; just be careful to only shake a few examples out of the bag.

The Dawn of Everything is a big book, with many theories considered, but the authors give appropriate attention to Matilda Joslyn Gage (1826–1898),[6] an "anti-Christian" who "posited the universal existence of an early form of society 'known as the Matriarchate or Mother-rule', where institutions of government and religion were modelled on the relationship of mother to child in the household" (p. 215), and to archaeologist Marija Gimbutas, of whom they write: "if you read the book of Gimbutas—such as *The Goddesses and Gods of Old Europe* (1982)—you quickly realize that their author was attempting to do something which, until then, only men had been allowed to do: to craft a grand narrative for the origins of Eurasian civilization" (p. 216). That grand narrative involved a pre-historical European civilization where the people were largely peaceful and worshiped female goddesses.[7] Neither Gage nor Gimbutas managed to penetrate the public or academic consciousness to any degree.

Archaeological finds in Central Europe show "how the apparent uniformity of the Ukrainian mega-sites arose from the bottom up, through processes of local decision making. This would have to mean that members of individual households—or at least, their neighborhood representatives—shared a conceptual framework for the settlement as a whole" (p. 295). The idea that food surpluses led to specialization and social stratification is a "compelling story. It is also quite true when applied to our present-day situation. . . . However, almost none of the regimes we've been considering in this chapter ['Why the State Has No Origin'] were actually staffed by full-time specialists" (p. 428). Priesting and fighting were seasonal activities, to be engaged in only when farming was slow.

Even the narrative of "imperialism" ecological or otherwise, the authors continue, might be better understood as a synthesis because . . .

> we are generally taught to think of the French political philosopher Charles-Louis de Secondat, Baron de Montesquieu as the first to build an explicit and systematic body of theory based on the principle of institutional reform with his book *The Spirit of the Laws* (1748). By doing so, it's widely believed, he effectively created modern politics. The Founding Fathers of the United States, all avid readers of Montesquieu, were consciously trying to put his theories into practice when they attempted to create a constitution that would preserve the spirit of individual liberty, and spoke of the results as a "government of laws and not of men."

As it turns out, precisely this sort of thinking was commonplace in North America well before European settlers appeared on the scene (p. 481). The authors intimate the possibility that Montesquieu might even have attended a political conference with the Osage and inculcated some of his ideas from them.

Finally, having presented evidence for a new history of humanity, the authors speculate as to why this new conception of human societies has gone unseen for so long. "We eventually came to realize that this reluctance to synthesize was not simply a product of reticence on the part of highly specialized scholars, although this is certainly a factor. To some degree it was simply the lack of an appropriate language. What, for instance, does one even call a 'city lacking top-down structures of governance'? At the moment there is no commonly accepted term" (p. 522).

A lack of appropriate language and symbols is very frequently a problem for relatively new fields of analysis; while anthropology and archaeology are not new, the attempt to synthesize fields, which is a requirement for this kind of thinking, is. With an understanding of this, and a basic framework for understanding *The Dawn of Everything*, a way to further the civilization conversation becomes clarified.

CONTINUING THE CIVILIZATION CONVERSATION

Questions about humanity's interaction with civilization have attracted some of the world's best minds, and the field of work is synthesizing into something impressive. *The Dawn of Everything* is unquestionably an important book, but the authors write as if they were trying to smash an existing paradigm rather than make an important contribution to the conversation; this approach limits the effect of their work because it caused them to make caricatures of important arguments, to overlook the importance of historical context beyond anthropology and archaeology, and to miss a key conclusion of their logic.

The Dawn of Everything is laced with a sarcastic wit which, while entertaining when Graeber aimed it at worthless bureaucrats and corporate lawyers in his previous book, works less well when addressing serious arguments like those made by Diamond and Pinker. This is not because the sarcasm reads badly (Graeber will forever be the smartest kid in class, sitting in the back, raising his hand to ask a sarcastic question and make the class laugh) but because the tone sometimes forces the authors into a Hegelian trap.

By attacking the accepted wisdom, the authors too often construct caricatures of the arguments put forth by other scholars, and thus end up arguing with opponents rather than conversing with colleagues. In addition to tracing the development of guns, germs, and steel, Jared Diamond wrote extensively about the native societies in Papua New Guinea,[8] where he lived and researched for a number of years, and his 1999 article, "The Worst Mistake in the History of the Human Race"[9] (the mistake being civilization), could have been foundational for Graeber and Wengrow's argument. They break Diamond's life's work into straws, select just a few, and then build and burn a strawman.

The authors criticize Steven Pinker for focusing on prehistoric skeletons that show evidence of violent death, while not focusing on other forms of anthropological evidence that show the opposite. But Pinker is aware that there are prehistoric skeletons that show evidence of having been cared for just as surely as there are skeletons that show evidence of violent deaths. Pinker's thesis deals with large-scale trends in data, not individual data points, and he has argued that already existing human impulses toward nonviolent behavior have been expanded by enlightened forms of centralizing governments.

The authors gently ridicule Frances Fukuyama for his history of political order, where they might have instead found much of value in Fukuyama's argument about how criminal organizations, like the mafia, can sometimes develop in the absence of a more centralized legitimate state. Such an insight might have been useful when applied to certain types of prehistoric evidence.

Very late in the book, Graeber and Wengrow write about the impact they believe their book will have:

> No doubt, for a while at least, very little will change. Whole fields of knowledge—not to mention prestigious research grants, libraries, databases, school curricula and the like—have been designed to fit the old structures and the old questions. Max Planck once remarked that new scientific truths don't replace old ones by convincing established scientists that they were wrong; they do so because proponents eventually die. . . . We are optimists. We like to think it will not take that long. (p. 525)

Might it be suggested that talking to other scholars who are interested in the same topic, rather than declaring them to be wrong and implying that the science might advance when they die, could help to facilitate new understandings?

There are times when Graeber and Wengrow's background as anthropologists and archaeologists seems insufficient for providing context to the historical movements they discuss. For example, on the topic of Rousseau's essay *Discourse on the Origins of Social Inequality*, they write:

> Rousseau's essay is undoubtedly odd. It's also not exactly what it's often claimed to be. Rousseau does not, in fact, argue that human society begins in a state of idyllic innocence. He argues, rather confusingly, that the first humans were essentially good, but nonetheless systematically avoided one another for fear of violence. As a result, human beings in a State of Nature were solitary creatures, which allows him to make a case that "society" itself—that is, any form of ongoing association between individuals—was necessarily a restraint on human freedom. (p. 64)

Rousseau's argument about human nature must be understood in the context of Christian history. To expand upon the authors' metacognitive themes, we might ask "what are the origins of the question about the question of human nature?" The answer to that is unique to Christian theology. The edifice of the Catholic Church was built upon the notion of a "sinful nature" that had been bequeathed to humanity via the Garden of Eden. Humans, taught the Church, were born bad and could only be redeemed through the Seven Sacraments, aka the "good works" of the Church. In 1517, Martin Luther agreed that humans were born bad, but believed "good works" to be all but useless for salvation, because faith alone could redeem humanity.

The Christians who "discovered" Native Americans after 1492 thus were predisposed to ask questions about human nature and saw Native societies as examples of what would happen to a human population deprived of salvation, hence the assumption that native pagan rituals were evil. In the 15th and 16th centuries, only Christians, upon encountering a New World full of people would have thought to ask a question about human nature. The Chinese Treasure fleet (1405–1433) came into contact with "pre-civilized" groups on Indo-Pacific islands, but the question of human nature seemed not to have materialized, probably because the Confucian Chinese saw their fleet as a way of superimposing their value system (the father is the head of the household, the emperor is the head of China, and China is the head of the world) on the Indo-Pacific.

In the same way that John Locke used secular philosophy to justify a religiously motivated Glorious Revolution (1688) in England, and thus create an Enlightenment foundation for the American and French Revolutions, Rousseau was secularizing the religious concept of human nature and using it as a way to critique civilization, and to begin by stating that human nature is bad would have marked him as a theologian. This is important because as Graeber and Wengrow write:

> Rousseau's model of human society—which, he repeatedly emphasizes, is not meant to be taken literally, but is simply a thought experiment—involves three stages: a purely imaginary State of Nature, when individuals live in isolation from one another; a stage of Stone Age savagery, which followed the invention of language (in which he includes most of the modern inhabitants of North America and other actually observable "savages"); then finally, civilization, which followed the invention of agriculture and metallurgy. Each marks a moral decline. But, as Rousseau is careful to emphasize, the entire parable is a way to understand what made it possible for human beings to accept the notion of private property in the first place. (p. 65)

What the authors missed is that Rousseau created an Enlightenment mythology that took the place of Christian mythology's "Garden of Eden" with "original goodness" taking the place of "original sin." In the same way that the Church redeemed original sin, civilization corrupted human nature. While Graeber and Wengrow asked the question of "from where did the question about the nature of inequality come from?" again, they did not then ask, "from where did the question 'what is human nature' originate?" It's an equally interesting question that provides a new insight into the conversation.

Furthermore, although the authors are seeking to overturn the received anthropological and archaeological narrative, they do so by accepting the accepted "Hobbes vs. Rousseau" narrative of the Enlightenment. But, just as there are alternative ways to interpret archaeological and anthropological evidence, there are also alternative interpretations through the Enlightenment.

By building on the work of Matilda Joslyn Gage and Marija Gimbutas, one could create a narrative of civilization where hunter-gatherer civilizations were ruled more by feminine characteristics such as cooperation and peaceful conversation, while civilization itself has traditionally favored more masculine characteristics such as aggression and violent confrontation. Graeber and Wengrow's most important contribution is to assert that civilization "got stuck" in a hierarchical mode at some point, but they did not see that there is a way of viewing the Enlightenment that provides a means back to the cooperative matriarchal forms of politics that could have governed so many early human societies.

If we accept that civilization has been a bad deal for women, and the fact alone that seven centuries of Chinese foot-binding probably crippled about two billion women should be enough to prove the assertion, then the rise and development of feminism as an ideology should be seen as the main Enlightenment narrative. Everyone quotes Hobbes, but why not Mary Astell (1666–1731) who wrote "But the scripture commands Wives to submit themselves to their own Husbands. True; for which St. Paul gives a Mystical Reason (Eph. V. 22 & c) and St. Peter a Prudential and Charitable one (I Pet. Iii), but neither of them derive that Subjection from the Law of Nature" (p. 564).

This may be the single most important sentence that anyone ever wrote. Astell is saying "The Bible says you can oppress women, but how does this Enlightenment concept of the Law of Nature justify it?" Rousseau answered in his 1762 novel, *Emile* by saying, "When women become strong, men become still stronger; when men become soft, women become softer; change both the terms and the ratio remains unaltered."[10] In other words, the Law of Nature justifies the subjugation of women because boys are stronger than girls.

Graeber and Wengrow don't cite Mary Wollstonecraft, probably because she only features in the traditional narrative of the Enlightenment as an early women's rights advocate, but Wollstonecraft arguably had more of value to say about civilization than either Rousseau or Hobbes. In her masterpiece, *Vindication of the Rights of Women*, she wrote:

> In the first place, the opinion in favour of the present system, which entirely subordinates the weaker sex to the stronger, rests upon theory only; for there

never has been trial made of any other: so that experience, in the sense in which it is vulgarly opposed to theory, cannot be pretended to have pronounced any verdict. And in the second place, the adoption of this system of inequality never was the result of deliberation, or forethought, or any social ideas, or any notion whatever of what conduced to the benefit of humanity or the good order of society. It arose simply from the fact that from the very earliest twilight of human society, every woman (owing to the value attached to her by men, combined with her inferiority in muscular strength) was found in a state of bondage to some man.[11]

In Wollstonecraft's theory, civilization is an extrapolation of male physical strength over women. If there is truth to that, then civilization "got stuck" in a mode that rewards masculine values over feminine values, and if that is the case, then we might need a new narrative, one where the Protestant Reformation, Western literature, the Enlightenment, and Western science (being the giver of the birth control pill) are resynthesized to see how feminism emerged. Feminism, then, would be the means of rebirthing the more egalitarian societies that Graeber and Wengrow draw attention to.[12] Redirecting the civilization conversation requires taking the same kind of approach to history and philosophy that Graeber and Wengrow have taken to anthropology and archaeology.

Accepting this, we then have questions that need answered. For example, men and women show a great degree of sexual dimorphism, with men possessing about 80% more upper body strength than women. What this indicates about our prehistoric past is not as important as the questions it raises about the present: Is sexual dimorphism incompatible with civilization? If so, should we try to solve this incompatibility biologically like we solved the problem of excessive women's pregnancies? Should our culture accentuate aggressive male behavior through competitive sports, aggressive policing practices, and hierarchical corporate culture? Or should we encourage cooperative activities, counseling and support systems, and more egalitarian forms of decision making and resource allocation?

Graeber and Wengrow's thesis can be described as such: early civilizations were like large and varied cooperative conversations. All of them, in time, came to be dominated by the same type of boorish and intimidating figure who shouts so loudly about how his presence is inevitable that no one else can get a word in. This is an important contribution, and it raises the possibility that, if we can rethink early civilizations and create new pathways of understanding through history, we might be able to conceptualize a future where human civilization returns to the more cooperate, peaceful, and egalitarian roots. If civilization has forced us to be ruled by masculine virtues, then maybe we can redirect ourselves to a new *dawn of everything*, one that is ruled by the more feminine characteristics of cooperation and egalitarianism; we just need to keep the civilization conversation going until we find a theoretical understanding that allows us to get unstuck.

Graeber and Wengrow have not overturned an existing paradigm, but they have provided an important contribution to what may be humanity's most important conversation about who we are, where we came from, and where we're going.

NOTES

1. David Graeber and David Wengrow. *The Dawn of Everything: A New History of Humanity*. 2021. New York: Farrar, Straus and Giroux.
2. David Graeber. *Bullshit Jobs: A Theory*. 2018. New York: Simon & Schuster.
3. Jared Diamond. *Guns, Germs, and Steel: The Fates of Human Societies*. 1997. New York: W. W. Norton.
4. Steven Pinker. *The Better Angels of Our Nature: Why Violence Has Declined*. 2011. New York: Penguin.
5. Francis Fukuyama. *The Origins of Political Order: From Prehuman Times to the French Revolution*. 2011. New York: Farrar, Straus and Giroux; *Political Order and Political Decay: From the Industrial Revolution to the Globalization of Democracy*. 2014. New York: Farrar, Straus and Giroux.
6. https://en.wikipedia.org/wiki/Matilda_Joslyn_Gage
7. Marija Gimbutas. *The Goddesses and Gods of Old Europe*. 1982. London: Thames and Hudson.
8. Jared Diamond. *The World Until Yesterday: What Can We Learn From Traditional Societies*. 2012. New York: Viking.
9. Jared Diamond. "The Worst Mistake in the History of the Human Race." 1999. *Discover Magazine*, April 30.
10. Jean-Jacques Rousseau. *Emile or On Education*. 2013 edition. Chelmsford, MA: Courier Corporation, 573.
11. Mary Wollstonecraft. *A Vindication of the Rights of Men and a Vindication of the Rights of Women*. 2014 edition. Cambridge: Cambridge University Press, 137.
12. Chris Edwards. *Femocracy: How Educators Can Teach Democratic Ideals and Feminism*. 2021. Lanham, MD: Rowman & Littlefield.

This chapter reprinted from *Skeptic* 27(1) (2022).

Chapter 2

The Brain and Education

One of the great insights of modern anthropology is modern humans are hunter-gatherers who have adapted to civilization. Our brains and bodies react well to the types of relationships and activities that could be found in a hunter-gatherer tribe but are less well-adapted to relationships and activities that are recent products of civilization.

A few quick examples highlight this effect: babies learn to talk by being immersed in spoken conversation. Likewise, babies and children can "pick up" (notice the allusion to what pre-civilized gatherers do) social cues and sensory motor skills just by playing and interacting with other people. Spoken language and social interactions have very likely been a part of human societies for about 150,000 years.

Yet, children have to be "taught" how to read and write because the manipulation of symbols to resemble things or sounds has only been a part of human civilization for about the last 10,000 years. Modern mathematics, defined here as beginning with the invention of the symbol zero, has only been with humans for a little over 2,500 years. The manipulation of such symbols requires years of practice, and to be a truly efficient writer, reader, or mathematician, it will require immersion.

This is a well-known thesis about human learning but such an understanding, that we are hunter-gatherers living in an alien environment only recently constructed, helps to define the purpose of education. The human brain exhibits a capacity known to evolutionary biologists as *exaptation*, or pre-adaptation. This means that the brain can develop talents, such as playing the violin or mastering calculus, that are not natural to it. This likely means that, at some point in human history, the brain evolved an agility to immediately adapt to new environments and circumstances. The brain, when combined with a few other anatomical factors such as the voice box, opposable thumb, and a hyper-efficient cooling system (aka sweating), allowed for the development of modern humans and modern civilization.

From this insight, we can develop several important questions, but first it is important to develop the correct analogical framework. The brain is not really, as is often iterated, like a muscle. It is true that muscles can be built up and trained with excessive use, but the billions of neuronal connections in the human brain defy the easy comparison to a simple muscle. Both muscles and connections are strengthened with use, but neuronal patterns can form novel connections that lead to unique pathways through information.

Certain "learned" behaviors, such as the ability to complete calculus equations or write novels, represent functions that began with the neurocognitive clay of pre-adaptations, but were shaped into a skills set by constant practice. However, because human ancestors evolved in an unpredictable and dangerous environment that would require quick cost-benefit analyses in a variety of situations, the brain is quite effective at in-the-moment statistical analyses.

Much of modern learning theory is being conducted by specialists working in Artificial Intelligence (AI) and so much has been revealed about the brain by comparing the human mind to computer minds. In *How We Learn: Why Brains Learn Better Than Any Machine . . . for Now* (2018), Stanislas Dehaene writes:

> According to an emerging theory, the reason that our brain is still superior to machines is that it acts as a statistician. By constantly attending to probabilities and uncertainties, it optimizes its ability to learn. During its evolution, our brain seems to have acquired sophisticated algorithms that constantly keep track of the uncertainty associated with what it has learned—and such a systematic attention to probabilities is, in a precise mathematical sense, the optimal way to make the most of each piece of information. (p. xxv)

The totality of the brain's activities defies analogy, but individual functions can be understood analogically. One way to think of the brain is to consider the neuronal functions to be like a movie projector. The ability for neurons to create a mental image (the mind's eye) to foresee potential future scenarios might be likened to the capability to imagine scenes from a novel or scenarios from thought experiments. The ability to read fiction strengthens the same neuronal networks that allow for the projection of future possibilities or allow the projection of one's consciousness into another person's situation.

The primary justification for broad learning in the humanities is that the skill set derived from the process "transfers" to other subjects. The most vociferous critic of the American educational system, Bryan Caplan, specifically targeted the concept of "transfer" in his 2018 book *The Case Against Education: Why the Education System Is a Waste of Time and Money*. Caplan writes about how, despite the fact that students rarely demonstrate a mastery of content knowledge in standardized assessments, the educational community comforts itself with the mythology of transfer:

> ... the prevalence of "useless" subjects and scarcity of "measured learning is an illusion." That fact that you neither use nor remember your course work in history and science does not make your coursework a waste of time. Thinking—*all* thinking—builds mental muscles. The bigger students' mental muscles, the better they'll be at whatever job they eventually land. (p. 50)

Caplan then presents a research-based argument that debunks this claim; students almost never transfer their specific learning to a new situation. "As a rule," he states, "students learn only the material you specifically teach them ... if you're lucky" (p. 50). The difficulty of developing transfer skills in students might come from the fact that transfer is rarely taught specifically as a skill, but rather as a means of testing mastery of content. The top-down nature of education takes away from the natural process of making cross-curricular connections that can occur in more organic forms of learning.

Examples of a transfer skill in history might come from recognizing the similarities between historical situations. One example is to study the outbreak of the First World War in 1914. In that war, major powers confronted each other over a small region, Serbia, and the Austro-Hungarians issued an ultimatum to the Serbs. This can be compared and contrasted with the Cuban Missile Crisis of 1962 where the United States and the Soviet Union clashed diplomatically over the installation of Soviet missiles in Fidel Castro's Cuba.

Both scenarios feature weapons of mass destruction, both feature a small region that becomes a focal point for the international prestige of major and competing powers, and both feature an ultimatum. Why did war break out in the chronologically first case but not in the second? By contrasting the two, we can leave the similarities inside a mathematical parenthesis and factor out the differences. Those would be that in 1914: (1) No quick forms of international communication existed. (2) In 1914, the major powers did not possess weapons of the same destructive power that existed in 1962, and knowledge about the destructive powers of their weapons was less detailed than in 1962. (3) The Americans and Soviets in 1962 had the recent examples of two World Wars to guide their decision making.

The above example differs from traditional assessments of transfer because those assessments usually teach students a specific skill and then give them a sort of "masked" assessment that appears at first to be unrelated to the taught skill but is actually the same thing. Math story problems are notorious for burying fairly simplistic equations inside of scenarios, and students who learned how to cross multiply the numerators with denominators on either side of the equal sign might not recognize that this method can be used to determine that if 10 acres can support 100 bushels of soybeans, then 15 acres can support 150 bushels of soybeans.

Students who do understand this often do so because they are taught, at some point, the specific language of word problems. The ability to see how the mathematical formulas equate with the words is a skill. However, that skill might not correspond with the ability to understand that the equations might only lead to a probabilistic outcome. Actual yields of soybeans from 10 to 15 acres will not likely be exactly 100 bushels and 150 bushels, respectively, because of real-world factors like the effects of climate and bugs.

A student who does realize this might, at some point, study chemistry and connect that understanding about soybean yields to the concept of theoretical and actual yields that comes from the study stoichiometry (the field that mathematically predicts chemical reactions). The theoretical yield is what would happen if the chemicals reacted perfectly, the actual yield is what occurs when trillions of tiny particles collide randomly but make a probabilistic jerky movement in a single direction that can be predicted with fairly close accuracy. Why can they be predicted? Because of what statisticians call The Law of Large Numbers, which is that the more samples one has, the more likely the probabilistic prediction based on mathematics is to be true. Chemistry almost always deals with exponentially large numbers.

Continue asking questions and you will walk out of the frame of the game into the vast whiteness of epistemology. There you will find a few questions such as "how large can numbers be?" which will require you to answer other questions, such as "how do we define numbers?" And then you will look down and find that if you don't start building analogies and axioms under your feet pretty quickly, you will just keep falling.

But let's stay in the frame for the purposes of this book and analyze how the building of Artificial Intelligence has helped scientists and computer engineers to understand the brain. In the paragraphs above, you were invited as a reader and learner to connect abstract understandings and analogies in a chain of understanding that very quickly moved from a few basic facts into some of the deepest realms of philosophical thought. Artificial Intelligence cannot do this. Dehaene writes:

> Most artificial neural networks capture only the very first stages of information processing—those that, in less than a fifth of a second, parse an image in the visual areas of our brain. Deep learning algorithms are far from being as deep as some people claim. According to Yoshua Bengi, one of the inventors of deep

learning algorithms, they actually tend to learn superficial statistical irregularities in data rather than high-level abstract concepts. (p. 28)

What is the significance of "high-level abstract concepts"? Let us examine one of humanity's most useful intellectual creations: calculus. Calculus need not be learned to its highest levels for someone to see the importance of its concept. One's thinking can benefit from simply understanding the structure and purpose of calculus. The structure is a method for measuring the fluidity of propulsion, and Newton specifically was able to solve Zeno's famous ancient Greek paradox by developing the calculus.

Zeno liked to flummox his listeners by asking questions about motion and distance. To paraphrase, if you could imagine a woman in her backyard with 10 ft between her and a tree and then imagine her crossing 5 ft toward the tree, then 2-1/2 ft, then 1-1/4 ft, etc., it becomes apparent that there is a theoretical infinity of halves between her and the tree. At any given moment, to measure the woman, she needs to be paused, and from that still state, it would be impossible to measure her movement or speed.

One answer to the problem of Zeno's paradox is to measure the distance traveled over a period of time. In basic physics, Distance equals Rate multiplied by time ($D = R \times T$). Rearrange that to Time multiplied by Rate equals Distance and then divide the Rate on both sides and Time equals Distance over Rate. Thus, if we know that it takes the woman 3 minutes to move 3 ft, she is moving 1 ft per minute. This is an average of her movement, but will not tell us how fast she is moving at any given point, because she might start slowly and then begin to accelerate. The equations of calculus allow for precise measurements of movement and speed by narrowing the focus of the equations as close to zero (but not touching zero) as is possible.

What was just presented is a framework for understanding calculus, not the application of the equations themselves. Just understanding the framework can provide a thinker with an application. Just being aware of what calculus is and does, that it measures fluid movement rather than binary position can be important. It might make the thinker less trusting of either/or arguments, or create a nuance to study controversial subjects such as abortion or gender, where life/not-life and male/female characteristics might prove to be ethically troubling.

The mastery of calculus and its equations become necessary at the level of actual application. In his book *Infinite Powers: How Calculus Reveals the Secrets of the Universe* (2019), Steven Strogatz writes of how calculus was applied to the study and treatment of HIV/AIDS. In the 1980s and 90s, a primary question about HIV regarded the "asymptomatic" stage, when those afflicted with the virus could go for many years without feeling the effects.

Strogatz writes that their medical researches questioned this period of viral dormancy, wondering if it was analogous to how chickenpox viruses sometimes "sleep" within cells for decades. This quote describes how Dr. David Ho (who had a physics background) and a "mathematical immunologist" named Alan Perelson managed to solve the problem. When it was discovered that, even in asymptomatic people, HIV reproduced exponentially, then the immune system must be working hard to keep the appearance of health. Strogatz writes:

> In a 1995 study, [Ho and Perelson] gave patients a protease inhibitor, not as a treatment but as a probe. This nudged a patient's body off its set point and allowed Ho and Perelson—for the first time ever—to track the dynamics of the immune system as it battled HIV. They found that after each patient took the protease inhibitor, the number of virus particles in his bloodstream dropped exponentially fast. The rate of decay was incredible; half of all the virus particles in the bloodstream were cleared by the immune system every *two days*.
>
> Differential calculus enabled Peterson and Ho to model this exponential decay and extract its surprising implications. First they represented the changing concentration of virus in the blood as an unknown function, $V(t)$, where t denotes the elapsed time since the protease inhibitor was administered. Then they hypothesized how much the concentrations of virus would change, dV, in an infinitesimally short time interval, dt. Their data indicated that a constant fraction of the virus in the blood was cleared each day, so perhaps the same constancy would hold when extrapolated down to an infinitesimal time interval dt. Since dV/V is the fractional change in the virus concentration, their model could be translated into symbols . . . (pp. 220–221)

The equations, mostly involving exponents and natural logarithms, that Drs. Ho and Perelson used to study HIV replication would not be beyond most high school students in advanced classes. Their genius was not in the mastery of the calculations but in the realization that HIV's dormant stage could be understood through the concepts of exponential growth followed by logarithmic removal (the virus being the exponent and the immune system being the natural logarithm).

Through the collection of data, and then application of a mathematical model, a better image of how HIV manifests itself during the dormant phase emerged. The virus was not hibernating; it was being evenly matched by the immune system. Strogatz explains it in this way:

> In the asymptomatic phase . . . there is evidently a balance between the production of the virus and its clearance by the immune system. At this set point, the virus is produced as fast as it's cleared. That gave insight into why the viral load could stay the same for years. In the water-in-the-sink analogy, it's like what happens if you turn on the faucet and open the drain at the same time. The water will reach a steady-state level at which outflow equals inflow. (p. 222)

This case exemplifies how knowledge is learned and applied. To just know that calculus is the antidote to binary thinking is one level of knowledge, to understand its calculations is another, and then to see that calculus could be applied to the mystery of the asymptomatic phase of HIV infection is another.

Strogatz explains a relatively complex mathematical problem by creating an analogy. The analogy of a faucet being turned on while the drain is open is easy to visualize. Then, he invites the reader to see that HIV infection created no symptoms for years because of the same reason that a sink with the faucet running does not fill up with water if the drain is open. Almost always, the most brilliant explanations are simple.

The implication of this analogy is that if the drain closes, then water will quickly overflow in the same way that if the immune system weakens, removing the logarithmic function, then the virus replicates exponentially. This understanding then led to a new medical intervention: antiviral drugs needed to be administered in heavy doses during the asymptomatic phase as a reinforcement to the immune system and not only with the manifestation of symptoms.

Laid cleanly out like this, the process seems obvious, but this is an illusion similar to what occurs when a novice math student watches a skilled teacher work neatly through a problem, and the student feels a sense of understanding. Often, that sense of understanding dissipates when the student is required to make an application to a comprehensive set of questions.

The application of the calculus to HIV required the development of a specific kind of attention. Dehaene writes:

> . . . our attention solves a very common problem: information saturation. Our brain is constantly bombarded with stimuli: the senses of sight, hearing, smell, and touch transmit millions of bits of information per second. Initially, all these messages are processed in parallel by distinct neurons—yet it would be impossible to digest them in depth: the brain's resources would not suffice. This is why a pyramid of attention mechanisms, organized like a gigantic filter, carries out a selective triage. At each stage, our brain decides how much importance it should attribute to such and such input and allocates resources only to the information it considers most essential. (p. 148)

While it is interesting to learn that calculus was applied to the understanding and treating of HIV, it may not be a fact that sends many people into an in-depth study of calculus toward mastery. Studies of attention spans reveal little, the dynamics of what can grab and keep attention are influenced by too many variables, but educational researchers do know about the importance of paying attention for the purpose of learning.

Video games, slot machines, and social media tend to absorb attention but do so by prompting the human body to release small doses of dopamine in response to levels completed, small-money wins, and the accumulation of friends, likes, and shares. Systems such as this can hold attention spans but confer little in the way of skill development. Gamers who spend multiple hours perfecting their abilities to win online wars are developing rudimentary skills but not the kind of complex cognitive connections that lead to useful insights.

Attention by itself certainly is not enough to foster deep education. Personal interest in a subject seems to be a key component of developing attention. This brings up the notion that students might be free to learn about a subject until it meets their level of interest. This is not to say that schools could not enforce a certain base level of knowledge about government, mathematics, geography, and reading comprehension but that base level of knowledge could and should be quite limited.

Again, it's important to return to the question, "what would you do if you needed to learn something?" If you had a pair of owls nesting in your backyard, and then became interested in their mating and hunting habits, would you need to master ornithology or even need to know the skeletal structure of the owls, or would a library book and a few online tutorials satisfy your curiosity? If a student develops an interest in *Romeo and Juliet*, this does not mean she will be interested in *Hamlet*, so why study it beyond the student's interest?

Part of the reason this might sound counterintuitive to the education process is because state academic standards tend to be created by experts in the various fields and field experts very frequently exhibit what Steven Pinker calls the "Inside-outside" problem, which is sometimes less generously referred to as "intellectual idiocy." This is the inability of people who are educated in a subject to understand that other people who are not educated in a subject are not familiar with the concepts and terms. Academic content standards tend to reflect the body of skills and knowledge that chemists, historians, mathematicians, etc. believe should be mastered to become a practitioner in that field.

A better system would allow students to study within a field until their level of interest became saturated. The objective here is to create learners who understand how to (A) become interested in something intellectual and (B) learn how to satiate that curiosity by accessing resources. The hope is that such activities will not be limited to just the years that he or she is in school.

There is no need, in an era where education for its own sake is readily present and nearly free, to put so much pressure on students in the years of their childhood and early adulthood. There is nothing at all preventing a student who fails to learn quadratics at the age of 16, from learning how to use the quadratic formula at the age of 40. It is hard to pay attention to the content you are not interested in, and it is impossible to learn deeply without that attention.

The rest of this book will describe the problems with the current educational system and will explain how those problems can be fixed with a Mastery-Learning Model. However, before moving on to these portions of the book it is important to address the concept of "partial-learning" because a shallow understanding of concepts can create havoc on internal mental processes. For example, let us analyze the First Law of Thermodynamics.

Mathematically, the First Law of Thermodynamics is expressed as $(\Delta) U = Q - W$. This means that the change in internal energy is equal to the Heat added to the system (Q) minus the work done by the system. In other words, Work creates Heat. Now, this concept becomes easy to explain because people heat up when they run and engines need to be cooled. Then it becomes apparent that stimulated particles create heat and this will be observed every time. It is a law after all.

The example of the First Law of Thermodynamics demonstrates how a mathematical understanding of something can be translated into a common-sense perception of reality. Likewise, the Second Law of Thermodynamics states that the universe tends toward entropy, or disorder. It is possible to understand this law mathematically as well, especially when applied to something like the sun's level of radiation output. However, it may take a while to realize that *everything* is radiating, and that radiation is itself a form of degeneration.

From that understanding, one can now see how night-vision goggles work. Instead of capturing the radiation of the sun as it bounces off objects, night-vision goggles detect the direct radiation coming from living bodies. We judge elements on the periodic table by how quickly they radiate away, with elements that have long half-lives radiating at a slower pace than those with shorter half-lives. Batteries run on entropy and are "dead" when entropy's movement is finished. At a deeper level still, we might detect that the word "energy" is really just used to describe how another object's entropy can be temporarily captured to make movement. (That is, the sun is radiating due to entropy, and living organisms on Earth temporarily capture that entropy.)

Even at that deep level of understanding, a student may not apply the specific point of convergence between the First Law of Thermodynamics and the Second Law of Thermodynamics. Having realized that "work creates heat" in so many circumstances, you may not have thought to ask "if work creates heat, then why doesn't heat create work?" It is, after all, the movement of particles that creates the heat, but the opposite is not true. Consider this passage from the classic text *Elements of Chemical Thermodynamics* (2005) by Leonard K. Nash:

> We have another conviction scarcely less intense—the conviction that the future will not repeat the past, that time unrolls unidirectionally, that the world is getting

on. This second conviction finds quantitative expression in a second principle of thermodynamics. Entropy (Gr. *Entrope; en, in* + trope, turning) is the state function distinguished by this second principle and, by always increasing in the direction of spontaneous change, the entropy function indicates that the "turn" taken by all such change. The foundation of thermodynamics occurred little more than a century ago, precisely when Clausius first brought together the two principles he later stated in the aphorism:

Die Energie der Welt ist constant.
Die Entropie der Welst strbt einem Maximumu zu

If a speeding lead bullet is stopped by an unyielding (and thermally insulated) sheet of armor, the gross *kinetic energy* of the bullet is converted into internal energy that manifests itself in a rise of temperature. But we never find that equal bits of lead, heated to the same temperature, suddenly cool down and move off with the velocity of bullets—though such a development would be perfectly compatible with the first principle of thermodynamics. Here is a striking but not atypical example of the entirely excessive degree of latitude left open by the first principle, which fails to exclude a great variety of changes never found in practice. As chemists we seek to predict the direction in which a reaction would proceed in reaching equilibrium, but either direction is equally compatible with the first principle. Only with the acquisition of a second principle can we put arrows into our equations when the reactions are tried. (p. 56)

In this dense paragraph, the reader can marvel at how Nash's mind works in complex ways as he draws upon his interests in chemistry and etymology to ask a question that can be paraphrased as "if work creates heat, then why doesn't heat create work?" A bullet that is "speeding" is working and the kinetic energy that is causing it to move then gets converted ". . . into internal energy that manifests itself in a rise of temperature." But, if one just heats a bullet up, then temperature rise will not manifest itself into kinetic energy.

The First Law of Thermodynamics by itself in no way forbids heat from creating work; it is only when the Second Law of Thermodynamics gets applied to the question of "if work creates heat, then why doesn't heat create work?" that the impact of the Second Law makes itself apparent. Because systems tend towards entropy, heat dissipates and objects tend towards coolness. This happens because order always loses to disorder and heat is a byproduct of the kinetic movement that can temporarily create order, and the kinetic energy itself is merely the temporary capture of entropy from another object. Once this is understood, the principle can be seen in virtually everything.

Let's go back to the beginning. In 1824, Sadi Carnot (1796–1832) published *Reflections on the Motive Power of Fire* where he noted that energy was always lost in any machine interaction. Since "energy" is the temporary capture of another object's decay it follows that:

> The result of these first operations has been the production of a certain quantity of motive power and the removal of caloric from the body A to the body B. The result of the inverse operations is the consumption of the motive power produced and the return of the caloric from body B to the Body A; so that these two series of operations annul each other, after a fashion, one neutralizing the other.
> The impossibility of making the caloric produce a greater quantity of motive power than that which we obtained from it by our first series of operations, is now easily proved. (p. 19)

If energy is always lost in an interaction, that produces heat (hence, the motive power of fire) which is what makes a perpetual motion machine impossible. This seems obvious, but its connection to mathematical analysis is more complicated. Consider this lengthy but necessary passage from Ananyo Bhattacharya's *The Man From the Future: The Visionary Life of John von Neumann* (2022). Bhattacharya's explanation of the development of quantum mechanics under the work of Niels Bohr and Werner Heisenberg is as clear as any ever written. Based on this premise: "Excite atoms, by vaporizing a sliver of material in a flame or passing a current through a gas, and they will emit radiation" (p. 31). He follows up with:

> Bohr had proposed these sharp spikes in the spectrum of radiated light were caused by excited electrons tumbling back to the ground state of an atom, in the process emitting light waves with energy equal to the difference between the higher and lower orbits. Heisenberg accepted this but he rejected the physical implications of Bohr's model—electrons had never been seen spinning in orbits around an atom's nucleus (nor would they be). Heisenberg instead stuck to the observed facts. He showed the frequencies of atomic emission lines could be represented conveniently in an array, with rows and columns representing, respectively, the initial and final energy levels of electrons producing them. When written like this, the frequency of radiation emitted by an electron falling from energy level 4 to 2, for example, would be found at row 4, column 2 of his array. But since electron transitions between different energy levels appeared to take place more or less instantly, there was no way to know whether an electron had jumped to its final state directly or passed through an intermediate state on the way. According to the laws of probability, the chance of two transitions occurring one after the other is equal to their individual probabilities multiplied together. To find the overall probability of all possible translations easily, Heisenberg arranged the individual transition probabilities in an array too, and multiplied rows and columns together. When he did so, he discovered a strange property of his arrays: multiplying one array, A, by another, B often gave a different answer from multiplying B by A. This troubled him because he

knew ordinary numbers did not behave in this way. As every schoolchild learns, multiplying 3 by 7 gives the same answer as multiplying 7 by 3. Mathematicians say multiplication is commutative because the two numbers can be multiplied in either order: A × B = B × A. But this was not the case with Heisenberg's arrays. They did not commute. (p. 32)

Mathematics exists in a Platonic realm, and there 3 times 7 can equal 7 times 3. However, since quantum mechanics predicts a heat loss in any interaction, any mathematical interaction designed to signify a quantum interaction must replicate the change. In quantum mechanics, an interaction can go forward but not backward. Or, as Nash said, work creates heat but heat does not create work. Therefore, 7 times 3 is not the same as 3 times 7. Matrix algebra, as tedious as it is, reflects a forward-moving quantum state. (In a strange way, this can actually be felt because a piece of paper is slightly warmer after the pencil creates friction while writing the equation, and so is a hand calculator after using energy to create the calculation.)

That particular example is content specific, and even though the First and Second Laws of Thermodynamics are both easy to understand and easy to find examples for, the question that Nash asked only became apparent after a genuine mastery of the concepts. Still, if this example seems too esoteric, then consider two items that most people come into regular contact with: a clock and a ruler.

A clock is just a ruler bent into a circle; that simple observation eludes most people who encounter clocks and rulers on a regular basis. The reason for that is because the mind separates the clock into a sphere for "time-keeping" and the ruler into a sphere for "distance-measuring." In medieval Europe, the ruler came first to create a centralized standard of measurement and this was part of a package of agreed upon measurements in weight and length.

If a ruler could be used to measure distance, then why can't a clock be used to keep steady movement in a world where movement tends to be chaotic? The realization that a clock is measuring movement, or at least providing steady-state movement as a reference point for comprehending real-world "chaotic" movement, then creates a series of analogies that shape how we think about physics; Einstein theorized that in the same way that your experience of distance differs depending upon speed, so too does your experience of time.

The study of one thing sometimes brings a greater level of understanding to another, seemingly unrelated thing. Let us return to the analysis of how calculus was used to create better treatments for HIV/AIDS. In the case of HIV, medical scientists misdiagnosed the "asymptomatic" phase as being analogical to the dormant phase that many other viruses exhibit. Only after calculus was applied to the phenomena did a more accurate diagnosis create better cures.

Can understanding calculus and HIV lead to a new process in foreign policy toward genocide or foreign conflicts? Currently, the United States and the United Nations wait until horrific events begin to occur and then debate, often to absurd levels while people die, whether or not the specific events of murder in a specific country actually meet the definition of genocide. Similar policies exist toward war in the Middle East, where American and/or UN intervention only occurs after the outbreak of hostilities, if ever.

This "treat-the-symptom" type of policy almost always leads to an aggressive intervention, too late in the process, that causes more damage to the situation. Almost no American president or foreign policy advisor can break out of the "bomb the problem away after the fact" form of intervention. What if foreign policy analysts identified certain regions of the world, Taiwan, Hong Kong, the eastern Uighir region of China, the 38th parallel dividing the Korean Peninsula, the Kashmir region between India and Pakistan, Russia and Ukraine (as is now obvious), and the northern region of Nigeria as areas where a conflict might not be lying dormant but where active peace negotiations and diplomacy are acting as logarithms to the exponential forces that could lead to violence or genocide? If that was the case, then heavier doses of peace negotiation and diplomacy at that phase might keep the peace.

The problem then becomes one of political will. As is often pointed out, politicians rarely receive plaudits or votes for taking preventative action. Nobel Prizes are usually given out to diplomats who help stop an existing war, rather than those who prevent a potential war. Yet, it would be possible to develop an algorithm for categories that tend to lead to war or genocide and when enough of those categories start to converge, a preventative measure could be taken. This is similar to how protective AI can work, where sensors detect that a number of factors that can lead to accidents are coming together. Removing even one convergent factor (get the dog away from the cat before the cat walks under the ladder with the anvil on top) can prevent disaster.

This is how we *can* think and this is what education *can* do, but it currently is *not* at the core of the educational mission. Informal learning, driven by someone's personal interest and sustained with deep reading and study, simply is not a component of the current educational structure. The next chapter will explain why.

Chapter 3

The Seat-Time Model

One of the strange features of American student life is the "college acceptance letter video" where would-be collegians rip open a paper letter from their "dream school" and then begin shouting in excitement as if they have won a major award. One could easily imagine a student who was accepted, say, to the Stanford Psychology Department would be screaming in joy for the opportunity to learn from the great psychologist Robert Sapolsky. Yet, Dr. Sapolsky's best lectures are all available for free on YouTube, so why is going to Stanford for education so important?

Now, there certainly are answers to that. Stanford provides a campus experience, and the students there actually get to interact with Sapolsky during lectures. These are good answers, but the question then becomes "how much is that extra experience, beyond the content, actually worth?" If I can watch the Sapolsky lectures for free on YouTube, access the papers he references for free on the internet, and check out the books that the students are reading for free at the library, then what is the cost of tuition for?

It is almost always useful to take a situation to its boundary conditions, where the differences are at their most extreme. A master's in business administration from Harvard Business School costs about a quarter of a million dollars. What do students in an MBA program do for 2 years that is worth a quarter of a million dollars? The answer to that, as detailed by Duff McDonald's damning and excellent *The Golden Passport: Harvard Business School, the Limits of Capitalism, and the Moral Failure of the MBA Elite* (2017), is that Harvard MBA specializes in business and ethical case studies.

High-quality case studies, created by experts in the fields of philosophy and ethics, can be found for free on the National High School Ethics Bowl website that is run by the University of North Carolina. Podcasts and essays on ethics are available, again for free, through websites maintained by the Prindle Institute for Ethics at DePauw University. There is no doubt that the Harvard MBA program offers a better overall experience in the study of case studies than any program of self-study could offer, but the question becomes "is the Harvard MBA program a quarter of a million dollars better than these free resources?" If not, then what exactly is the high cost for?

This becomes harder to explain with an economic model because education itself as a commodity is still not well understood. Consider this quote from *The Golden Passport*:

> While the fight for the number one spot atop the seemingly endless number of business school rankings is a highly competitive one . . . there is one category in which [Harvard Business School] has no rival: the opulence of its campus. Both the architecture and the grounds give off a strong scent of money and power, a fact that surely plays some part in the faculty's periodic displays of tone-deafness about the state of things outside its gates.
>
> For those people who have a connection with HBS, whether they are students, alumni, or faculty, everything *really is* just fine in the world. For all the criticism that HBS deserves to have lobbed its way, it really doesn't have any dissatisfied customers. It is a rare HBS graduate who regrets having gone to the School, the faculty (and their research budgets) is the envy of the business school universe, and the CEOs and companies that trade money for respect with the School could hardly hope to find a better cheerleader than they have in HBS.
>
> While there are many reasons one might choose to attend HBS, one of the most common is the opportunity to supercharge one's earning ability. At this point, the business school rankings track average starting salaries of schools' graduates down to the penny, but those numbers vary from year to year. And salary isn't what matters to these people; wealth is. And if you want to become wealthy beyond belief, you could do a whole lot worse than spend two years at HBS. (p. 530)

McDonald makes it pretty clear that the cost of the "golden passport" that is a Harvard MBA has little to do with the actual education; the real commodity is the access to the major financial firms that take MBA students out for lunches, and who mine HBS for talent. Students in the MBA program are buying access to an elite financial world. That much is clear, but what is less clear is this: why do financials find it important to hire talent from the Harvard MBA programs? One can assume that the Harvard MBA is not exponentially greater than those offered by plenty of ordinary state institutions (one can only dress up case studies so much).

The best answer to that might be that, in the same way that some social media stars are "famous for being famous" that a Harvard MBA is "prestigious for being prestigious." Once this is understood at the boundary condition, then the principle can be seen as economic and social force all the way through the educational structure. The problem with a commodity based on "prestige" is that the concept itself is fragile, not unlike confidence in cryptocurrencies.

Two problems make the current educational structure deeply unstable. The first is a massive, and almost certainly temporary, financial bubble based on the high value placed on higher education and the credentials that institutions of higher education confer. The second is a crippling teacher shortage.

To explain the first problem, a short analysis of the history of higher education must be established. The medieval university of Western Civilization created the concept of exclusivity in education because, prior to the dissemination of the printing press in the mid-15th century, compiled historical knowledge was rare. The Quadrivium, created by Boethius (died, 524) centered around a largely bookless set of skills. Charlemagne (r. 764–814) started a process of book-collecting and translation that turned the monasteries of the Middle Ages into scriptoriums. Only people with the skills of literacy could access the books of scriptoriums, and because the handling of books causes gradual damage to them, only the elites were allowed to handle the books.

After the printing press, the Protestant Reformation, and the Scientific Revolution, books became plentiful, cheap, and accessible to a large percentage of newly literate subjects and citizens. Higher Education remade itself in the 18th century, in Germany, when the finest German universities created the modern Ph.D. and declared their new function to be in the creation of new knowledge through the use of the scientific method, rather than only through the study of old knowledge. This concept created the modern research university and added a "commodity" to higher education that can be understood as the resources to answer novel questions through the collection of scientific evidence.

The "research university" model spread to French medical schools during the Napoleonic era and then to the United States in the early 20th century. By then, old and established Ivy League universities cultivated elite groups of men for leadership roles in society and became places of carefully guarded privilege. But as 19th- and 20th-century progressivism began to affect the American intellectual elite, a dichotomy emerged in American education: the desire to educate the masses with equality while at the same time preserving the Ivy League universities as safeguards of the American elite.

That first impulse manifested itself, in 1909, with the publication of the Harvard Classics, otherwise known as Dr. Eliot's Five-Foot Shelf of Books, a collection of the 50 greatest works considered to be necessary for a comprehensive education. The entire series of books would have been prohibitively expensive (although, the entire collection can now be bought in an e-edition for the Kindle for less than a dollar) and the classics are not really accessible to people with low literacy skills or low levels of sustained concentration, but a motivated learner without money could likely have found the works in a public library.

Up until 1969, the Ivy League universities almost uniformly kept women out of their undergraduate programs. State universities had admitted women for nearly a century by that time, but the primary reason was that those universities could not afford to turn away the tuition dollars that female students brought with them. The Ivy League's refusal to admit women was a way of signaling that America's elite campuses did not need that extra money.

More will be stated about this shortly, but the Western education systems were designed to provide universal education for the masses for the purpose of creating future democratic citizens and employable future taxpayers, but also for the purpose of determining who should go on to become the leaders in politics, the academy, and business. Because the true experts in the various fields were on the elite college campuses, an "elite" education was a rare commodity and it could not be wasted on individuals who were not intellectually capable of benefitting from that education.

That was the basic justification for the strict entry rules into the major universities, and the entire structure was held up by the conceit that schools and testing systems should be involved in measuring *potentiality*. In other words, the pyramidal structure of K–12 education was designed to systematically determine who was most likely to succeed in institutes of higher education. This was part of the function of Intelligent Quotient tests, the SAT, and the use of grade point averages to measure one's ability to learn; and this ability to learn was something that prestigious institutions regarded as important because those educational institutions possessed a precious commodity of genuine education.

Taking 2010 as a more-or-less arbitrary start date, access to elite education suddenly became available to anyone with an internet connection and the development of mass-produced hand-held supercomputers (a better term than cell-phone) meant that just about anyone could access the lectures of elite professors at just about any time and for a very low cost. The best stuff on YouTube, however, is the high-value content, particularly in the teaching of mathematics and the sciences, that is being created for a general audience of students.

Educational institutions have not adjusted to the rapid dissemination of this content, and a gap has developed between the market value of just learning something and the value of learning something for the purpose of attaining a degree. The gap continues to widen, bubble like, at a rapid rate but will eventually right-size, or pop when the top of the bubble is reduced to the same horizontal plane as the bottom of the bubble.

This spread of educational content has happened so quickly that it has created a temporary gap in the price of the commodities and the "right-sizing" of educational prices and availability will create several forms of restructuring. If the purpose of schools and the testing industry is to measure a student's potentiality to learn, then it needs to be recognized that there are two ways to measure potentiality:

1. The potential to learn can be measured through IQ tests and general skills tests like the SAT. Although such standardized tests should not be considered as measures of innate intelligence (a reified concept according to Stephen Jay Gould in his 1981 classic *The Mismeasure of Man*), studies show there is a reasonable connection between success on these assessments and general academic performance. However, any test of potentiality before the act of actual content learning will always be statistically imperfect. Which brings us to the second point.
2. The other way to measure someone's potential to learn is to actually see whether they learned something. Only variable factors in the assessment prevent such a method from being 100% effective. For example, in April, if we want to measure whether someone is capable of learning how to solve math problems involving quadratic functions then we can just teach someone how to solve math problems involving quadratic functions. If, by May, then the person can solve them we can then retroactively state with confidence that this same person had, in April, the potentiality to learn how to solve math problems involving quadratic equations.

If #2 seems absurd, this is because there is no point in measuring potentiality after the fact. The whole point of measuring potentiality is to select those with the most potential. If high-quality education can be made available to everyone, then it becomes possible to measure who learned the content after the fact. If a high-quality education can be made available to everyone, then the ability to measure potentiality becomes moot. Now that it is possible to provide access to high-quality education and accurate assessments regarding content and skills, the measure of potentiality is pointless. Rather than take an IQ test to see how well you *might* learn, study the content and skills, and then see how you *did* learn.

And this means that an entire structure designed around the measure of potentiality and the exclusiveness of elite education is obsolete. The effects of the global pandemic in 2020 and 2021 rendered the seat-time model an absurdity, if not an abomination.

The 19th-century novelist Grant Allen once stated that he "never let my schooling interfere with my education." The quote was later, and falsely, attributed to Mark Twain but one could imagine that an autodidact like Twain would have agreed with the sentiment. The difference between schooling and education is a phenomenon that has been understood and lamented for a while now, but the pandemic has crystallized the difference. Put simply, education has never been cheaper or more accessible, bottoming out at zero dollars in many cases, while the cost of a college or university education continues to expand. This does not happen with other commodities; it is not the case that the cost of gasoline drops to nearly nothing per gallon at one station and also rises to a thousand dollars per gallon at another.

If the higher education system is actually selling education, then this disjunction in prices creates an economic paradox. Fortunately, paradoxes are usually flaws in our understanding and a logical analysis of these phenomena can create some novel solutions for the educational system.

In a 2011 book titled *Academically Adrift: Limited Learning on College Campuses*, Richard Arum and Josipa Roksa examined the effects of the Collegiate Learning Assessment, a test on general critical thinking skills, that was given to a statistically valid sample of college students at the beginning of their freshman year and then again 2 years later. That assessment indicated that 45% of students in the sample made no improvements at all in their thinking skills during their time at college.

Yet, despite such poor educational outcomes, the cost of a college education at both public and private institutions has risen by more than 25% (adjusted for inflation) between 1978 and 2018 (https://cnb.cx/3q671Ro). Based on simple supply-and-demand theory, one would think that the development and spread of the internet and the free or extremely inexpensive educational sources available there would have brought the price of a college education down. While it has always been the case that most local libraries contain the same books that are taught at Harvard, it was not always true that someone with academic interests could access the course of the best scholars.

But in the current era, the same forces that are making entertainment cheap and accessible are doing the same thing with actual education. The best example of the difference between learning and education, or the difference between actual education as a commodity as opposed to "credentialism" which is when educational institutions confer degrees and licensure, can be seen by analyzing the "Teaching Company's" Great Courses (now Wondrium) series. The Teaching Company was founded in 1990 by Harvard alum Thomas M. Rollins, who had enjoyed watching a rare video-taped lecture series and decided to market high-level lectures through CDs and DVDs.

The business model was immediately profitable and, in the 1990s, the Teaching Company sold its content for about the same rate that universities charged for credit hours. A single course could run upwards of 48 lectures, came with a lecture outline book, and could be watched or listened to as many times as the purchaser chose. Although the courses were often discounted, the list price for a longer course could run as high as $700. Now, for about $20 a month, one can purchase a "Great Courses Plus" subscription. This means that a year's subscription to access all of the courses costs about one-third as much as the purchase of a single course in 1990 and that is without adjusting for inflation.

It costs virtually nothing now to record content, and a hyperlink to YouTube can be made for free and spread exponentially at no cost. It is no longer necessary to create DVDs or CDs, and the cost of physical shipping has evaporated into satellite sharing. The Great Courses offers expert professors, easy-to-understand packaging, and continuity but excellent content is available for free on YouTube as well. Need to know how to calculate the force of friction for a physics course? YouTube it, or ask Google Images for the formula. Interested in feminism and literature? Type it into YouTube. Want to know how to complete the square so that you can solve questions involving conic sections? You know where to go.

If you are interested in YouTube tutorials on mathematics, stay after "class" and look at the comments sections. Many, or most, are variations on the theme of "in five minutes, I learned more from this video than I did in an entire semester with my college professor/teacher. Thank you!" Every tuition and tax payer in the United States should consider this: students everywhere are paying thousands of dollars to access a university education but getting their actual learning from free YouTube tutorials. YouTube is providing the skills that help students pass the assessments that lead to university credentials. This is an enormously expensive disjunction with a simple and cost-effective solution that will be discussed in the next chapter.

For math education, about $15 a month buys access to the website StudyPug.org where subscribers gain access to a direct education on how to solve problems across math and science. While "The Great Courses Plus" is just a series of recorded lectures, StudyPug.com offers math questions coupled with a clickable link where the solution is explained. Students can learn at their own pace and not feel shy about asking that a lesson be repeated, and not have to worry that an instructor is becoming impatient with them. One can easily imagine the same setup being created for, say, the study of Shakespeare, where a student reads a passage and then clicks on a link showing a dramatization of the scene and/or a scholarly interpretation of it.

Free websites like physicsclassroom.com or flippingphysics.com can give students a thorough education at any time, and in any place where the internet is available.

When the 2020 COVID-19 pandemic caused almost all American schools and universities to close, education had to be delivered online. Suddenly, the American educational system, at all levels, was divested of its Ivy Walls, its massive stadiums, and its cushy dorms. It was stripped down to the delivery of content and skills, and it was revealed to be lacking. An October 2020 *Guardian* article highlighted the problems of "Zoom University" (https://bit.ly/3fIluNh). If students were studying in relative isolation by zooming with a college professor, then why should that experience be so vastly more expensive at a private or public university when a better educational experience could be attained through online educational courses?

The pandemic did not create the problem; it highlighted the commodity disjunction between schooling and education. Bryan Caplan's 2018 book, *The Case Against Education: Why the Education System Is a Waste of Time and Money*, is a woeful work, filled with statistics about how uneducated the American public is. Caplan builds on a theory established by five Nobel laureates in economics that connects a collegiate degree with "signaling." A college degree may not equate with a person's acquisition of knowledge or skills, but it does signal something about the person's background and behavioral "norms." The real value of the degree, these economists contend, is not in the actual attainment of education but in the personal character traits with which the degree tends to be equated.

Caplan's book is thought provoking, but the central thesis contains two flaws: First, although he is a sociologist, Caplan continually questions the direct importance of studying the humanities. The problem with the universities, according to him, is that professors design courses around their own interests rather than society's needs. This leads students to study Shakespeare rather than technical writing. The flaw here is in not seeing the general cognitive effects that come from deep reading; education is not always linear. Second, Caplan does not consider that a student might be paying for a precious commodity: time. It takes time to study and learn, and in some circles that time must be "bought" in a socially acceptable way.

Ultimately, higher education is moving in two different directions, and two books detail these separate trends: *Unacceptable: Privilege, Deceit and the Making of the College Admissions Scandal* (2020) by Melissa Korn and Jennifer Levitz (both journalists for the *Wall Street Journal*) and *Grasp: The Science Transforming How We Learn* (2020) by Sanjay Sarma (who led the Open Learning Department at the Massachusetts Institute of Technology at the time of his book's publication). *Unacceptable* could just as easily have been titled *Inexplicable*. The authors introduce us to a world where wealthy parents consider their children's success to be a social credit:

> A fracas once shook Larchmont Charter School in West Hollywood after a staff member there had the gall to start an advanced kindergarten reading group, recalls publicist Alison Graham, who lives in the high-end Hancock Park neighborhood and had a child in the school. Some parents whose children

weren't advanced readers erupted. The weren't about to let other kids get further ahead of theirs in *The Cat in the Hat* or *Chicka Chicka Boom Boom.* (p. 3)

At the turn of the 21st century, as the children of baby boomers prepared to enter college, such competitive attitudes about educational attainment meant that:

The moment had arrived for an aggressive college counselor. Baby boomers' children were graduating from high school in droves, ratcheting up competition for spots at elite and even formerly middling schools. Just over three million Americans graduated from high school in 2002, an increase of more than 21 percent in just a decade. (p. 28)

Colleges benefitted from the glut of applicants in several ways: as demand went up, colleges could turn away more students and this raised the prestige level because college rankings and reputations are based on exclusivity. This kind of environment allowed someone like Rick Singer—orchestrator of the college entrance scam that landed several celebrity parents in jail—to show parents how to cheat the system by falsifying applications or by making "contributions" (many seemed a lot like bribes) to universities. Singer would sometimes help parents push high school guidance counselors and administrators to move soon-to-be-college-applicants into the "best" teacher classrooms.

One of Singer's clients, the actress Lori Loughlin, has become the exemplar of the whole scandal. Loughlin and her fashion designer husband Mossimo Giannulli spent half a million dollars to falsify the application so that their daughter, Olivia Jade, could enroll at the University of Southern California. Olivia Jade had already established herself as a teenage social media star and it seems unlikely that she needed a college degree for her profession. It's difficult to understand why her parents wanted Olivia Jade to promote herself on social media in a USC dorm rather than in her own bedroom, except in the context of her parents seeing their daughter's entry into the university as a social signal.

The most perplexing part of this scandal comes if one asks the question "what was wrong with what Olivia Jade was doing?" Her lifestyle posts on YouTube promoted exercise, healthy eating, and beauty products. Had she presented a business plan and dressed up her concept in terminology "using a free social media platform to promote a healthy lifestyle to pre-teen and teen girls, and to use product placement for environmentally beauty products to meet the profit margin" and then implemented her plan, then she would have likely been praised, but since she intuitively worked her way into a (very crowded) market, there was apparently a feeling that her work could not be taken seriously unless she had a degree.

Fortunately, for Olivia Jade, the transgression of her parents did not destroy her business model. Olivia seems to have played no part in the admissions scandal, and she has rebranded her lifestyle vlog. She often films herself hanging out with friends in vacation-like locales, a brilliant signal to young people that it's okay to calm down and enjoy the day sometimes.

Olivia Jade's business model brings in about a million dollars a year. To reiterate a point; she is essentially a social media "reality" star who promotes a positive lifestyle to teen and tween girls. She handles herself well with the media and seems to have forgiven her parents for the scandal. In other words, she is the most mature person involved in the whole mess. Her situation seems an exemplar for much of what is wrong in the education system: adults not recognizing that the interests of young people can be developed into business models that make a contribution to society.

The reason that there is prestige in the college admissions process, according to Sanjay Sarma in *Grasp: The Science Transforming How We Learn* is because the educational establishment is designed to "winnow." Sarma sensibly rejects the education-as-factory analogy that too often upends discussion about education, and states flatly that "Once you realize how education systems are set up not just to nurture, but also to cull, you begin to see it everywhere. We winnow in how we test, and we winnow in how we teach." He goes on to write that, "Right from the start, a whole slew of access-related factors cut short education journeys before they even begin" (p. xv).

To repeat an earlier point; since the development of the medieval university, students in Western civilization have had to go and find education at certain elite institutions. The difficulty of access meant that only those students deemed most worthy could actually access those institutions, hence the development of prestige that came with being someone who made it through the winnowing process.

Sarma's book may be the most important work on education written this century; he correctly sees that educational materials are usually developed without a thought given to how students actually learn. Sarma is also sensible, writing "I believe the best education is still human-to-human education" (xxvi), but understanding that technology can expand the best educators to connect with more students. Unlike Caplan, Sarma does not see a liberal arts education as a waste; he draws upon the work of neuroscientists to conclude that "of all the things we do, reading is spectacularly, perhaps *uniquely*, demanding" (p. 73). One might then ask "Why don't schools just require that students read a lot?" which would further Sarma's point that education can be cheap and simple. In fact, Arum and Roksa determined that of the college students who did increase their critical thinking skills after 2 years of college, the commonality was that those students took classes that required considerable amounts of reading and writing.

The major difference between Caplan and Sarma is that while Caplan sees winnowing and signaling as the central features of the educational system, with actual learning occurring only incidentally, Sarma thinks that education can be salvaged. Referring to Course 2.007, a project-based robotics course that concluded with a competition that did not affect grades, he writes:

> Today, as I ponder how to avail a truly effective education to as many people as possible, I keep returning to Course 2.007. The way it separates the school's winnowing function from its teaching function—stripping apart two aspects of education that have been glued together for over a hundred years hints to at least one viable way to rethink the winnower and make education substantially more inclusive. (p. 230)

In his role as the head of the Open Learning Department at MIT, Sarma needed to separate those two functions of education so that he could take the actual educational value (learning), at its vastly lower market rate, and make it accessible to people around the world. This needed to be done in a way that was useful for students and to the communities they lived in. An online service like StudyPug.com confers only teaching, but not credential. Students use the service so that they can do better in the courses that confer the credential. MIT, however, has the value of its name and reputation. From this, came the birth of one of higher education's most impressive ideas, the MicroMasters:

> We wouldn't mess with MIT's bachelor's degree—in many ways a sacred object—nor with our PhD. The master's degree, however, was intriguing, featuring a number of arbitrarily stuck-together elements that, with a little care, could be teased apart. What if, I wondered, we were to crack a master's program in half, putting the parts most suited for online learning on the internet and reserving for campus those parts requiring face-to-face interaction? (p. 232)

The result was the creation of Massive Open Online Courses (MOOCs) that could be shared across the world, completed in about a year and a half, and the student could either take just the classes for $1,000 or take the classes and sit for the final exam for an extra $200, for a degree that conferred the prestige of MIT.

The MicroMasters at MIT creates the potential for a truly monumental shift in the economics of higher education. Universities have traditionally measured their value, particularly through bizarre journalistic "rankings" that use a complicated set of metrics mostly based on *exclusivity*. Exclusivity is determined largely by how many applicants that a university turns away. The development of exclusivity into a high-value market commodity has been one of the most destructive features of American life, and that will be explained in the next chapter. However, if elite institutions shift the market value of their prestige toward the demonstrable mastery of skills and away from the exclusivity of the entrance, then this changes the entire function and dynamic of education. Most significantly, it changes the economic structure of education.

One should never make definite predictions, but it is hard to see a future scenario where the cost of college education can continue to rise. Former students in the United States drag around an accumulated $1.7 trillion in debt and the vast majority of this debt is accrued by paying for learning that is available for free. What explains this economic paradox? Economically, students are not paying for learning but they are paying for the prestige of the institution and the level of an institution's prestige is directly connected to its exclusivity. (There are numerous problems with exclusivity as a commodity, but it will suffice here to point out that exclusivity as a concept is not trending well in the early 21st century.)

It is probably best to think of high educational prices as a temporary mass economic delusion. Mass economic delusions, as noted by William J. Bernstein in *The Delusions of Crowds: Why People Go Mad in Groups* are usually associated with market "bubbles," which can be understood as temporary inflations based on an excess of exuberance, or systemic "everybody-is-doing-it" thinking in the lending sector. Cryptocurrencies, especially bitcoin, are especially susceptible to economic delusions. Bernstein writes that ". . . one of the cardinal diagnostic features of a bubble is a vehement response to skepticism . . . the excitement surrounding cryptocurrencies, of which bitcoin is the exemplar, seem to exhibit all the signs and symptoms of earlier financial manias" (p. 387).

How can it be that the tuition paid for higher education amounts to a delusional bubble when it is the case that those institutions have, for hundreds of years, provided a stable base for educational training and development of a professional class? The answer to that has to do with the emergent technologies that have made education cheap and readily accessible.

What changed, and therefore created the bubble, is that about 2010 most Americans had ready access to YouTube tutorials and after the pandemic, just about anyone with an internet connection can access online educational platforms. An economic bubble can be created by the sudden drop in the price of a commodity if it takes a while for the attitudes and expectations of consumers to change. Bubbles usually form from the ground up, but sometimes the bottom can drop and form one as well.

To create a hypothetical analogy, if electric cars become feasible for long distances and cheap to make and to fuel with battery chargers, this would not collapse the oil market immediately. In the short term, gas prices might rise as oil drillers might cut back in anticipation of a drop and as the die-hard drivers of gasoline-powered cars refused the transition, but the rise in gas prices would be a temporary bubble before the price of gas collapsed.

This analogy is not exact, because people putting gas in their vehicles are not subject to a delusion, but an educational industry where institutions are "prestigious for being prestigious" creates a delicate market very susceptible to a shift in consumer attitudes. A critical mass of bright young people who decide to forgo the debt-inducing process of earning a bachelor's degree in favor of attaining skills for free while earning money at a job could collapse the higher-education market.

Financial delusions usually occur when there is an overabundance of excitement over something new, not an irrational attachment to something old. This is what makes the delusion more difficult to see, but if prestige is connected to skill attainment rather than to the exclusivity of the institution, then the market will shift quickly.

The development of the MIT MicroMasters creates a question. Why, if a degree from MIT costs so little, is it the case that a bachelor's degree from a state school costs so much? Given that Sarma's work explains away the economic paradox of higher education, then what is the future? Here are three possible scenarios:

1. *The Bubble Bursts.* Not all signaling is bad, and one could argue that when parents and students pay college tuition they are, in part, buying time to study in a way that is socially acceptable. The phrase "I am in college" confers a very different meaning than "I am learning physics online in my parents' basement." But at some point, the ever-expanding cost of winnowing and signaling, all done while in the conspicuous comforts, tricked-out dorms, exercise rooms, and flamboyant sports programs that are all but completely disconnected to the educational mission of the university, will finally burst not unlike the housing market did in 2008. College and university bureaucrats have taken advantage of the economic demand created by the children of baby boomers and pushed the going rate of a college education to its maximum point. If the bubble bursts, the well-paid university bureaucrats who facilitated the problem will be retired and, like the housing marking lenders, will face no repercussions for their actions. Unlike the lenders, however, universities are unlikely to be bailed out when vastly cheaper educational alternatives exist.
2. *Employers Move to a Skills-Based Application Process.* If a company wants to hire someone who can code then it can either ask to see an applicant's college degree and take a school's word for it, or they can just ask the applicant to, you know, *code.* If employers start moving to rigorous testing methods rather than focusing on degree requirements, then young people might see the direct value of real education and be able to attain it at a market level. An applicant would not need even $12,000 worth of MIT prestige, just whatever the pure education itself was worth.

This shift is taking place and coming along with an and/or process of businesses creating internal degree programs. To use just one example, Google has developed a career certificate program that essentially functions as an in-house university where the certificate holds the same professional clout as a university master's degree but for vastly less cost. More broadly, it would not be hard for an educational consulting company to audit a business and then, working from that audit, develop educational structures specifically designed to assist the company. Instead of employees doing work for their job and doing separate work for their degree, an employee could complete work for her education that is directly related to her job. In fact, "higher degrees" in a structure like this might be only given out for products that made money and/or provided some kind of societal benefit.

3. *Elimination of the Bachelor's Degree.* This is more of a suggestion than a prediction, but it is the case that American universities are subsidized with tax dollars and universities are simultaneously damaging lives and economies by loading young people with debt while at the same time demonstrably failing to improve the cognition of students to a degree that would justify the debt. Surely, college can provide a number of benefits for young people beyond what being self-taught would supply, but how much should those extra benefits cost?

A basic undergraduate package of education can be delivered to students just about anywhere and for next to nothing. Moving away from a seat-time model (as Sarma suggests) to a skills-mastery model would allow students to enter into higher education at any time, for little cost, and without being intimidated by a university culture that might be alien. There really is no reason that universities could not eliminate the bachelor's degree and create, in its place, objective tests on reading comprehension, mathematics, history, geography, chemistry, and current events and use the results of those examinations to determine who can enter into graduate programs.

The best part about doing away with the bachelor's degree would be that it would also eliminate the National Collegiate Athletic Association (NCAA). Most conversations about the NCAA's inherent corruption revolve around whether or not top-level athletes should be paid, but the NCAA actually creates a mass-market for average athletes who possess an otherwise useless skill set (almost always involving the manipulation of an inflatable ball) that somehow is supposed to equate with a deservedness to be educated on a scholarship.

Competitive sports do much damage to university life, but football in particular creates a culture of idiocy and recklessness. One example that will serve many is the case of Darrel Hawkins-Williams, a defensive back for the Sam Houston University Bearkats. In a pandemic-makeup playoff game in May 2021, Hawkins-Williams dove at a James Madison University player and the two cracked helmets together. Hawkins-Williams scrunched his neck making the (probably illegal) hit, and then lay completely unconscious on the ground with his leg twitching. A stretcher carried him off the field with his neck in a brace. The game, of course, went on and Sam Houston won an improbable comeback. The website Texasfootball.com relates this:

> Down by 13 points, how the Bearkats players handled watching their teammate leave the field on a stretcher would decide whether their season would end on Saturday.
> The response was exactly what the Bearkats expected, rallying around their teammate by scoring the following 21 points to defeat James Madison 38-35 in the FCS semifinals.
> "All signs look good. That was a helluva hit," Sam Houston coach K.C. Keeler said. "That was emotional. I got emotional because these kids mean so much to us. When you see a kid go down like that, it's hard, and it was really hard."
> "The guys talked about seeing a guy putting his body on the line to make a play, and if he could do that, why can't we all do that?"

That's the lesson that the coach took from the game? A young man making an illegal hit on another player's head went down unconscious and Coach K.C. Steeler saw this brain and neck injury as a motivational moment to drive his players all to put their "body on the line to make a play." And the "all signs look good" comment showcases the coach's ignorance of the late-occurring effects that often accompany severe head and spinal cord injuries. His player is now at a significantly higher risk of developing both CTE and potentially ALS.

For what? So that Sam Houston can win a meaningless game against James Madison in a division that no one outside of the campus families cares anything at all about? So that the coach can pad his credentials while looking for a job somewhere more prestigious? Why do schools encourage young men to face a lifetime of neurocognitive oblivion in exchange for education?

Just a few months before that, at the Armed Forces Bowl, a brawl broke out between the players of Tulsa and Mississippi State. Among the kicks, shoves, and punches, a Mississippi State player not only gleefully kicked a downed opponent in the face and then ran off, but then created a video for social media where he seemed to rejoice. The Mississippi State coach, Mike Leach, responded after the game that, in paraphrase, he wasn't going to lose his mind over the fight because it was a football game and people get hit. In February of 2022, University of Michigan basketball coach, Juwan Howard, grabbed an opposing head coach by the shirt and then struck an opposing assistant coach in the face during the post-game handshake. He was suspended for a few games, but what other publicly paid employee could act in such a way and keep a job?

What is this? Why are institutions of higher education involved in subsidizing athletes, encouraging young people to sustain brain and spinal cord injuries, and providing national platforms for aggressive and idiotic behavior that provide no benefits to society? Young people can have fun and get exercise through cooperative work; there is no reason to pit middle schools, high schools, and universities against each other in mock combat. Human society faces genuine problems like nuclear proliferation and climate change and those problems will almost certainly be solved by implementing feminine virtues like communication and cooperation; not through an aggressive mock-up of pre-gunpowder battle charges.

In June of 2021, the U.S. Supreme Court declared that university athletic departments could now provide all the perks they want for athletes in the recruiting process. Most of the commentary about this focused on how the athletes deserve more in compensation for the revenue they generate, but the Supreme Court decision will likely destroy the NCAA. How will the full-tuition-paying nonathletes who make up the majority of the student body feel about watching students with more fast-twitch muscle fibers taking a limousine to class, or being provided with penthouse suite dorms and private chefs? How does privileging athletes help anyone learn anything?

By eliminating the bachelor's degree, it might be possible to finally escape the hold that competitive sports have on educational institutions and process. Let professional basketball and football organizations pay for their own feeder teams; there is no reason why tax and tuition payers should fund the building of elaborate sports stadiums when the National Football League and the National Basketball Association get to reap the profits from farming those NCAA programs for talent.

The economic paradox of modern higher education, where education gets cheaper while schooling gets more expensive, may be a temporary aberration. Unless other universities adopt MIT's innovative open-source model, the paradox will likely sort itself out, sooner or later, one way or another. If the purpose of secondary education is, in part, to prepare students for learning beyond K–12, then a shift will have to be facilitated at the lower levels as well.

Chapter 4

The Seat-Time Model and Society

The STM has metastasized across education and into the economy, which makes the model particularly damaging. When the housing market collapsed in 2008, the causes were generally linked to "predatory lending" or a kind of mass delusion amongst home-buyers who believed they needed to own a large home to keep up appearances. The role that schools played in the 2008 crisis has not yet been fully explored, although it should be because schools exert a powerful influence on property values. This economic fact must first be understood before the myriad problems of secondary education can be addressed and solved.

An April 2021 issue of the *Public School Review* (https://www.public schoolreview.com/blog/what-is-the-connection-between-home-values-and-school-performance) cites a study of the effects of public schools on property values, conducted by the National Bureau of Economic Research. That study determined that a dollar spent on public schools leads directly to a 20-dollar increase in home values. The *Public School Review* website also defines "good" school districts as those where the average standardized test score is 30% above the average. The site also includes this fascinating finding:

> A more recent study by the Brookings Institution found that housing costs tend to be higher in areas where high-scoring schools are located. The study, which looked at the 100 largest metro areas in the country, found an average difference of $205,000 in home prices between houses near high-performing and low-performing schools. Homes around high-performing schools also tended to be larger, with 1.5 more rooms than homes near low-performing institutions. In addition, the number of rentals in areas near high-performing schools is around 30 percent lower.

Although research on the specific numbers is not available, it might be worth looking at the number of school board members who list "real estate agent" as a profession. The National Association of Realtors includes an entire section on its website (https://www.nar.realtor/articles/serve-on-a-school-board) stating how important it can be for agents to be involved in the governance of local school districts.

A 2015 *Washington Post* article, titled "School Quality Has a Mighty Value on Neighborhood Choice, Home Values" included this very telling statement:

> Good schools are also a top factor among home buyers nationwide.
>
> The 2015 National Association of Realtors Home Buyer and Seller Generational Trends study found that the "quality of the school district" was the sixth-most-important factor influencing the neighborhood choice of home buyers around the country, but for buyers 35 to 49, the school district was the fourth-most-important factor.
>
> A recent Trulia survey found that 35 percent of Americans with children under 18 indicate that their "dream home" would be in a great school district, while 12 percent of those without kids have that same dream. However, when the study separated out parents by age group, 46 percent of millennials and 28 percent of Gen Xers with children said their dream home would be in a great school district.

"Good" school districts, and this should not be surprising, tend to attract young homebuyers who either have children or are planning to have children. Mayors, city council members, and business people who sit on the Chamber of Commerce tend to like to attract that type of clientele for obvious reasons: they pay taxes and spend money. In many ways, this property-values phenomenon is an inadvertent effect of the 2001 No Child Left Behind Act (NCLBA).

The NCLBA can best be understood as an attempt by the federal government to force a competitive-business analogy onto school districts. Test data would be treated like stock prices, and administrators empowered as executives. This analogy favored conservative visions of education and an inevitable aspect of the analogy was a "blame-the-teachers-unions" for failure mentality.

Conservative commentators are almost never comfortable criticizing school district management; perhaps they understand that their role is central to the economic development of a suburb or city. Anger at public schools then gets directed at unions that are somehow preventing the school district from being even better. The objective seems to have been to put school districts into a business-like competition, but to disallow the inevitable failures that occur in a business-like competition.

The NCLBA categorically failed to improve large-scale educational outcomes, but it did provide school districts with data that could be advertised.

And that data created a boon in property values for certain districts. The obvious correlation between the public's perception of school quality and the property values in a suburban neighborhood created intense pressures on school districts to signal success, prosperity, and happiness through sustained public relations campaigns. Schools, like corporations, require that employees sign a contract that forbids any public criticism of the district or school and condemns it as insubordination.

One side effect of such clauses is that teachers cannot effectively speak out against toxic and/or abusive behavior perpetrated by administrators. School districts function with a feudal model, where a school board hires a superintendent to act as the authority over the district. The superintendent presides over a court of bureaucrats (assistant superintendents, curriculum directors, and Chief Financial Officers) who dispense policy to building-level principals. The building-level principal then uses his/her bureaucracy (assistant principals, deans, etc.) to oversee the implementation of corporate policy in the classrooms.

This whole process is upheld by the mythology that administrators were the expert teachers who moved into leadership and sustain their authority with educational expertise. The fact is that, because of the feudal nature of school districts, there is nothing that connects a teacher's classroom job performance with his or her movement into administration. Because elementary schools tend to be smaller, teachers will have more contact with principals at that level and so the impact is more dramatically felt; at the high school level, teachers and administrators may rarely have personal contact with each other. A building-level administrator who taught physical education for 5 years, might, absurdly, be in a position of evaluating a physics teacher with 20 years of experience.

Data on the effectiveness of administrative evaluations of teachers tend to conglomerate K–12 institutions and that makes it hard to separate high schools from elementary schools, but overall the whole process seems to be misaligned with what researchers know about how teachers develop and students learn. Consider this passage from *8 Ways to Make Teacher Evaluations Meaningful and Low-Stress*, by Denisa R. Superville (2019):

> In the past, principals tended to have a laser focus trained solely on what the teacher was doing, every single minute of the visit—a by-product of what state evaluation systems asked them to do. But teachers, principals, and experts say that principals should pay attention to the classroom environment—what students are doing, what teachers are asking them to do, and the kinds of questions students are asking.
>
> Keishia Handy, the principal of Cole Elementary School in San Bernardino, Calif., uses five-minute sessions to pick up many cues about teaching by watching students.

"Are they using the academic language that is aligned to the content within the standards?" said Handy. "Are they asking questions that indicate that they're actually processing the information, or are they asking surface-level questions because they don't understand what's being presented? I'm also looking to see if they're using one another for resources, rather than having kids raise their hands and asking the teacher for help."

In this case, the principal is looking for factors that may have nothing at all to do with whether students are learning anything or not. Students may not ask questions for a variety of factors, with anxiety and the "spotlight effect" (the tendency of adolescents to believe that they are the subject of everyone's hyper-aware attention) probably foremost among them. The use of academic language and the willingness to ask other students or the teacher for help are not indicators of content processing.

The principal, in this case, is merely looking for indicators that students are being kept busy in a seat-time educational model and the indicators for teacher success are largely based upon a bias towards extroverted students and teachers. A quiet student processing information through silent deep reading would not help a teacher's evaluation in this case, although deep reading produces vastly more impressive cognitive effects than asking a question using "academic language."

To return to an earlier point, a student who played "World Map Quiz" on his phone for an hour in class each day would very likely know where all of the countries in the world were located at the end of the 6 weeks, but a student who plays a game on his phone for an hour during class would be unlikely to improve a teacher's score on a formal observation. Superville then quotes Robyn Jackson, "a former school administrator turned consultant" who advised:

> "Usually when we see struggling teachers, we give them feedback that says classroom management was a mess, planning was a mess, instructional delivery was a mess, assessing student performance was a mess," [Jackson] said. "Then we say, 'I'll be back in two weeks, that all needs to be fixed.' That's impossible, especially for someone who is struggling."

The truth is that school administration just is not very good at helping teachers who are struggling and neither are continuing teacher education programs. A 2012 paper titled "The Sheepskin Effect and Student Achievement: De-Emphasizing the Role of Master's Degrees in Teacher Compensation," written by scholars at the Center for American Progress on the effects of teacher master's degree programs found that, while almost all school districts gave salary increases to teachers with advanced degrees, that there was no evidence that teachers with those degrees actually improved student outcomes.

This finding has influenced state educational policy regarding teachers and compensation in both Indiana and North Carolina and is doubly flawed. First, student achievement does not only have to be defined by improved test scores; a teacher who engages students more effectively and makes the classroom more enjoyable while still getting students to the same level of proficiency might be considered to be teaching more effectively. Second, it might have been possible to create more effective forms of ongoing teacher education; compensation for advanced degrees did not have to stop entirely, but the elimination of financial benefits for teachers seems to have been the only conclusion drawn by the researchers and by conservative legislators.

After about the year 2000, the charter school movement emerged as a potential way around traditional school bureaucracy, but it soon became apparent that charters could not magically improve student outcomes. The real purpose of charters, which are not beholden to elected school boards, may have been to further empower the administrative class. In *Reinventing America's Schools: Creating a 21st Century Education System*, author David Osborne quotes Rene Lewis-Carter, a charter school principal in New Orleans on what she did as a principal that led to her winning the 2015 Louisiana Middle School Principal of the Year Contest:

> She did not mince words when explaining her success: "If something does not work for my children here at Behrman, be it a teacher, be it a textbook, I can get rid of it. I got to handpick teachers" . . . And those teachers "understood that things were different, that if they did not perform, they did not have to be here the very next day." (p. 40)

Later, she more succinctly stated ". . . For the first time I can tell a teacher, 'You know what, your teaching stinks,' and I'm not going to be served with a grievance" (p. 41).

Such an attitude is prevalent in all school reform models. One of the most influential books on professional development in the last 50 years has been 2004's *Whatever It Takes: How Professional Learning Communities Respond When Kids Don't Learn* by Rick and Rebecca Dufour, Robert Eaker, and Gayle Karhanek. The ideas in this work, thin to begin with, had to be thoroughly stretched to make it book-length. Essentially, the Dufours (it is not clear what the other authors added) suggested that teachers be put into teams called "Professional Learning Communities" and that those teams look at student work for the purpose of determining what classroom methods were working and which were not.

The authors then tacitly endorse a "leadership" model based on coercion and intimidation when they write ". . . the principals faced the challenge of one or more new staff members who were either aggressively or passively resistant to the new direction of their school" (p. 143). Then, a page later, they highlight this section in praise of a principal:

> Sale-Davis even went so far as to hand out transfer requests to all her staff, encouraging them to apply for a transfer if they were unwilling to embrace the ideas of consistent learning outcomes, common assessments, and collaborative culture. The faculty came to understand that the school stood for certain principles that every staff member was expected to honor. (p. 144)

Every staff member was expected to embrace a "collaborative culture" it seems, except for the principal who sought to implement a bland reform through an ostentatious display of intimidation. Principals and the administrative class have abused teachers for as long as there have been public schools. That history has been told in an excellent book by Dana Goldstein titled *The Teacher Wars: A History of America's Most Embattled Profession* (2015), and much of that history involves misogyny and mistreatment of female teachers by a mostly male, and almost entirely mediocre, administrative class.

Because of the feudal nature of a school district, and because teachers are disempowered and kept at the bottom of a chain-of-command hierarchy that disallows them from speaking publicly about school policy and largely prevents them from being protected from abusive and/or incompetent administration, the conditions are rife for abusive behavior in schools. Worsening the problem is the fact that building-level administrators quickly find that their reputation with the corporate office can be harmed by complaining parents, but not by unhappy teachers. In schools where the students are in competition for academic honors and for spots in elite colleges, this can create an environment where teachers see the administration only as the "muscle" that acts on behalf of parents.

Every school "reform" movement seeks only to remove teacher protections, eliminate the authority of elected school board members, and empower the bureaucratic class to "hire the best and fire the worst" teachers. This whole concept rendered the entire philosophy behind the NCLBA laughable (in a sinister way, think "The Joker") since the idea was to put school districts in competition, then have the "best" districts create a model that could be replicated. A school district that hires the best and fires the worst would succeed on a model that, by its nature, cannot be replicated. If a suburban hospital improved outcomes by attracting the best doctors from urban regions, this would not have a net positive effect on healthcare and would not be a scalable model of reform because there is no more a massive pool of highly effective doctors than there is of highly effective teachers.

This was never the point of either NCLBA or of the educational reform movements; the purpose seems to have been to empower and enrich the administrative class. The College Board, which oversees the SAT and

"Advanced Placement" tests at the high school level, typically nets well over a billion dollars and avoids taxation because of its status as a nonprofit. The business model is clever because the Advanced Placement tests for each subject area tend to be easily built and then they need only be copied and dispersed, then students pay up to about $85 to take the exam.

Why would students take the exams? Students get a cumulative score of 1–5 on the test, with a "3" being enough to count for a college credit in most states. A list of colleges that accept the AP score for college credit can be found here: https://pages.prompt.com/colleges-that-accept-2020-ap-credit#nochange. Why would a college accept the AP score as a college credit? Mostly they do so either because students with high AP scores tend to increase the all-important exclusivity of the institution or because the individual state law requires it. In the state of Indiana, for example, state law requires that any college which accepts state funding will have to accept an AP score of "3" or above for a college credit, although many colleges only accept those credits as electives.

At the start of 2021, the Speaker of the House for the Indiana General Assembly was Todd Huston. Huston, whose only experience as an educator came from his time as a bureaucrat in the Indiana Department of Education, possesses a bachelor's degree in political science and had a day job as an Executive Vice President for the College Board (where his compensation was almost a half a million dollars per year) and helped pass laws that created demand for Advanced Placement tests in the state. Huston resigned from the job in early 2022 when journalists pointed out that this support for a conservative curriculum bill for Indiana schools could be a conflict of interest.

Added to this problem is that peddlers of professional development can sell books, online modules, and programs to districts so that each school can check legal boxes for offering professional development and you can see how much money flows through school districts into private hands. More recently, fears of school shootings have created an industry devoted to selling "school safety" modules to districts. It is common for the creators of the modules to lobby state legislatures to pass laws where it becomes mandated that local school districts force teachers to engage with online learning modules about school shootings, how to administer CPR, and student mental-health awareness. One example of how private businesses make money off of this can be found here: https://www.safeschools.com/.

In many cases, the school-safety training seems to have gotten out of control. The purpose of the shooting seems to have been to remind these elementary teachers that if they failed to fight back against a shooter, then they would just be riddled with more bullets.

Whatever the problem, from mental health troubles to teen drug use, low literacy and numeracy levels, and school shootings, there seems to be a state-mandated online module that can be required of teachers that addresses the problem. The modules tend to come complete with easy-to-guess-the-answer multiple-choice assessments that indicate that the module creators don't really care whether anyone is actually paying attention to the content.

With this much money and political power invested in a traditional hierarchical system, it is little wonder that so little attention has been paid to the effects of how this structure abuses teachers. Only one significant study, completed in 2002 by Joseph and Jo Blase, attempted research into the topic of Principal Abuse of Teachers. Tellingly, the researchers had to rely on qualitative analyses of the topic because school districts do not compile data about abusive principal behaviors. Broad national research into teacher morale does not directly ask about teachers and their experiences with abusive administrators.

Their 2002 book, *Breaking the Silence: Overcoming the Problem of Principal Mistreatment of Teachers* laments that principal abuse of teachers is ". . . a problem for which there exists literally no research base." Yet, if their qualitative research provides a sample of a larger problem, then:

> It deals with a situation that has not been exposed to light, whose silence has been without challenge, and for which public and professional awareness, scrutiny, and improvement efforts have not been forthcoming. This information exposes what may be a surprisingly common problem that has alarmingly destructive effects on teachers as professionals and as people, one that reaches directly into classrooms to drastically undermine and even destroy opportunities for effective instruction and student learning. The powerholders who create this problem and those who collude by permitting it to continue are participating in a phenomenon that has the potential to devastate an entire school, even an entire school system, by relentlessly and unconscionably crushing its spirit and destroying educators' morale, commitment, trust, caring, hope, and basic human rights, including the right to respectful and dignified treatment. (p. 1)

Breaking the Silence details the emotionally abusive treatment that teachers too often suffer from when principals, cloaked in too much authority for too long, inject toxicity into schools and the very psyches of teachers. Lest anyone think that principal abuse stems from a desire by principals to force out "bad" teachers because the unions make it too hard to fire those teachers, the Blases are clear that the quality of the teacher seemed to be no protection against abuse. Celebrated "Teachers of the Year" were among the victims that the authors interviewed.

In a 2006 follow-up paper, "Teachers' Perspectives on Principal Mistreatment," for *Teacher Education Quarterly*, the authors included their definition of "emotional abuse" as ". . . the hostile verbal and nonverbal behaviors directed at gaining compliance from others . . ." and that includes a pattern of abuse. Again, the authors stated that ". . . theoretical or empirical work on abusive school principals is nonexistent" (p. 126). They wrote that any specific research on abusive principals tends to get lumped in with general research finding about "bad bosses."

The qualitative research by the Blases makes for depressing reading and the qualitative nature of the work makes it difficult, but not impossible, to assess the actual effects that abusive principals have on education or just how widespread the problem is. However, one of the teachers interviewed for the paper stated:

> I have lost so much of myself. The more bookwork, page work, and blackboard work that I do, the less alive the students seem, I can see a change. The light went out of their eyes. I was told I needed to control them rather than make learning a joint venture. I became a teaching box filling up heads with information so that they could pass the test. I want out (a veteran teacher). (p. 128)

I want out. Those three words echo across the profession, and when teachers leave it is usually because of unsupportive or abusive administration. A 2016 study by the U.S. Department of Education indicated that in the 2003–2004, 2007–2008, and 2011–2012 school years, 90% of teachers agreed that they were satisfied with their jobs. One of the findings was that in 2011–2012, about 95% of public school teachers who agreed that the administration in their school was supportive were satisfied with their jobs. This was 30 percentage points higher than teachers who disagreed that the administration was supportive (National Center for Education Statistics).

Teacher morale, as indicated by a survey in a 2008 MetLife study, indicated that 62% of teachers reported that they were "very satisfied" with their profession. Just 4 years later, that number fell to 39%, the lowest number that had been registered in 25 years. The same survey revealed that just over half of teachers are "very stressed" several days a week. The number of teachers feeling that way had increased by 70% since 1985. A separate survey indicated that about 25% of teachers are stressed about finding time during the day to use the restroom (https://www.theatlantic.com/education/archive/2016/02/what-if-americas-teachers-made-more-money/463275/). (When students must be supervised at all times it is impossible for a teacher to leave a class of students, and in some schools with block schedules the teachers do not get a preparation period every day.)

A report from the Alliance for Excellent Education stated that "over 1 millions teachers move in and out of schools annually, and between

40 and 50 percent quit within five years." While any author or researcher must be careful making assertions about a "teacher shortage" when there are 13,600 separate school districts in the country and where some subject areas are harder to staff than others, the best statistic likely comes from an EdWeek survey where local administrative personnel (those in the best position to answer) simply reply to a survey asking whether or not their school district is experiencing staffing problems. In 2021, two out of three districts reported that they were experiencing a shortage (https://www.frontlineeducation.com/blog/teacher-shortage-2021/).

The findings of the 2021 (and thus, post-pandemic) survey are worth quoting in full:

> While many rural school systems cited their location as a major factor behind their teacher shortage, districts in all settings are struggling. Teacher shortages are most common in urban school systems, with 75% of districts in cities of any size reporting shortages. In comparison, 65% of rural districts reported shortages, along with 60% of suburban districts.
>
> Across all settings, 44% of districts with shortages reported having difficulty filling vacancies across grade levels and subjects, while the remaining 56% reported only having shortages for specific positions. This suggests that the teacher shortage has worsened noticeably overall: in previous years, only about 34% of districts with shortages struggled to find applicants across different subjects and grade levels.
>
> The most common shortage cited should come as no surprise: 71% of districts with shortages find it challenging to find Special Education teachers. And as we have seen in previous years, the substitute shortage claims second place—though it is close to becoming the most common shortage.
>
> 67% of survey respondents reported a substitute shortage this year, which is in line with substitute shortage data from the Frontline Research & Learning Institute. It's possible that substitutes felt intimidated by the prospect of online and hybrid teaching or did not wish to risk catching COVID-19 from in-person classes. (Unfortunately, it's unlikely that the substitute shortage will disappear entirely, even after the pandemic.)
>
> Other top shortages are:
>
> - Secondary Math (reported by 46% of districts with shortages)
> - Paraprofessionals (35%)
> - Secondary Physical Sciences (26%)
> - Bilingual Education (25%)
>
> Some vacancies—such as Secondary Math and Sciences—historically have been hard to fill. However, the rise of the paraprofessional shortage is worth a discussion. It's possible that the paraprofessional shortage, like the substitute shortage, has worsened due to COVID-19.

This is just a look at temporary data about a problem that's growing worse. The teacher shortage has two major effects: (1) It makes it less likely that a student will encounter a professional educator with a stable sense of her career who can effectively educate students. (2) It renders all of the educational reforms instituted since NCLBA obsolete since all of those reforms are based on some kind of "hire the best and fire the worst" conceit; they are reliant upon a massive labor pool of highly qualified candidates to take the place of "the worst." Those teachers are not there, and evidence indicates that few young people are choosing classroom teaching as a future career.

The feudal nature of the American system will prevent a full-scale collapse, but a partial collapse or a direct reduction of educational services can be damaging to vast numbers of students. A meta-analysis of the research indicates that the weight of economic, social, and political expectations is putting too much pressure on individual classroom teachers. This creates vast levels of turnover and the teachers who do remain often carry around low morale with them and low teacher morale is connected to lower levels of student achievement.

It is telling that paraprofessionals and substitute teachers are in low supply, as these are very frequently jobs that attract retired people and parents who have children in the district. In rural districts, it's not uncommon for the local school district to be the single largest employer in a county. For parents and grandparents, the chance to be on a work schedule that affords time off at the same time as children or grandchildren can be powerful attractors. However, the conditions of the school have become so pressurized that shortages are severe for substitutes and aides. The 2020–2021 pandemic school year saw several school districts in the country "go virtual" because of substitute teacher shortages.

The whole structure is unstable and ineffective; the fewer teachers there are in classrooms, the more difficult it is to hold them accountable for good teaching practices, something that renders the administrative class as obsolete. And we haven't even talked about how all of this affects the students yet.

The STM is not good for learning and is not good for students in general and the reasons why will be detailed shortly. However, before explaining the problems with the STM, it is probably a good idea to start by answering the question that readers will likely ask immediately: "if the STM is so inefficient, then why is commonplace?" For the sake of brevity, the three main reasons for the continued use of the STM will be addressed here: The first is that the STM fits with the schedules of working parents. The second is that educational structures evolved with the STM which means that vast numbers of people are employed due to the inefficiencies of the system, and that employment is threatened by change. The third has to do with a suburbs-to-campus educational pipeline that has become the economic model on which the universities thrive.

It is beyond the power of individuals to fix the educational structures that they work in, so the purpose here is not to critique teachers, professors, or even administration, but to understand that the system persists despite these serious flaws because it does provide some level of service. To understand that is to embed those services into a more efficient MLM and, in so doing, eliminate the many problems inherent in the STM without taking away from the necessary societal functions performed by the status quo.

To address the first point; the STM probably persists chiefly because K–12 schools are safe places where children can be taken care of while their parents are working. During the 2020 spring term, virtually every school in the United States abruptly switched to virtual learning of some sort and many schools began the fall term of the 2020–2021 school year with either a fully virtual or hybrid schedule. This revealed that schools provide an essential function for the economy.

The economic and social effects of this shutdown were shocking; by February of 2021 labor statistics indicated that about three million women had exited the workforce (https://www.cbsnews.com/news/covid-crisis-3-million-women-labor-force/). For an economic theorist, it was easy to form a hypothesis. When the kids could not go to school, a parent had to stay home with the children and in most cases, this turned out to be the mother. Why it was that women, rather than men, tended to leave work to stay home with children should be a subject of great interest to sociologists, but for the purposes here, it is enough to say that huge sections of the modern workforce rely upon schools to take care of children during the working day.

When school boards approve calendars for the year, this creates a sense of stability for the working parents who live in the district and it becomes possible to make plans for childcare during the scheduled breaks in the school year. Activities associated with the school, such as sports and extracurriculars, create further regularity and keep young people in monitored activities.

The problem is that students then become a population to be managed at a large scale; schools need to avoid liability and students cannot go unmonitored. The reason that teachers frequently do not have time to use the restroom is because halls must be monitored during passing periods and students cannot be left unmonitored in classrooms. Students become subject to a surveillance state that restricts and monitors their movements even more than prisoners. One study found that, while inmates in correctional institutions receive about 2 hr outside each day, the average school child is outside for less than an hour (the study was intended to showcase a general lack of outdoor time, not just at schools). Almost no high schools plan regular outdoor time for students at all.

A 2016 article in *The Atlantic*, appropriately titled "When School Feels Like Prison," includes this passage:

> In December 2012, a Senate subcommittee was convened to examine the school-to-prison pipeline, a national trend in which overly punitive school discipline policies push students out of school and into the criminal-justice system. Among the witnesses at the first-ever congressional hearing on this issue was Edward Ward, at the time an honor-roll student in his sophomore year at DePaul University and a recent graduate of Orr Academy on the West Side of Chicago. He offered an eye-opening *first-hand account* of his high-school experience. "From the moment we stepped through the doors in the morning, we were faced with metal detectors, X-ray machines, and uniformed security," said Ward.
>
> Far from an aberration, what Ward depicts—public schools serving primarily black and other nonwhite students that rely on more restrictive security—is quite common, according to a new research paper from Jason P. Nance, an associate professor of law at the University of Florida Levin College of Law. Nance set out to find if there was a proliferation of school security following highly publicized school shootings like the tragedy at Sandy Hook Elementary School in Newtown, Connecticut. He discovered that many schools had intensified their security and surveillance of students, but the practice was not equally applied. Rather, schools with a preponderance of students of color within the school building were more inclined to adopt strict surveillance practices—metal detectors, locked gates, security cameras, random sweeps, and school police.

While the above might be an extreme example overall (although common for people in impoverished communities where a school-to-prison pipeline is just as common as the school-to-college pipeline is in the suburbs), students everywhere in the country have the same educational evolution from elementary through high school. As elementary students they are primarily with one teacher all day and get to know the same group of kids. Then in middle school or junior high, the elementary schools all begin to mix together and students often will switch teachers depending on the subject. By high school, the students are thrown together in a competitive environment with students they don't know who come from other "feeder" schools in the district. They switch teachers between three and six times a day.

The net effect of this constant monitoring is, to quote the title of an NEA study, *The Epidemic of Anxiety Among Today's Students* (2018). The article builds off of a 2018 Pew Study where, to quote the article "70 percent of teens say anxiety and depression is a 'major problem' among their peers." A further 26% defined it as a minor problem. The article then cites a 2011 study by the National College Health Assessment where about 75% of college students self-reported "overwhelming anxiety" a number that was "up from 50 percent just five years earlier . . ."

This should be no surprise given the immense pressure put on the years 14 to 24, where students are encouraged to believe that if they don't start exhibiting traits of either academic or athletic greatness, then they won't be able to get into good schools and have great careers.

This brings us back to the original question this book posed. "What would you do if you needed to learn something?" Does anyone learn exceptionally well shuffled from class to class in a highly monitored environment and then stuffed into a crowded room filled with strangers and directed by teachers with sometimes radically different approaches and expectations?

That inefficiency creates the second function of the STM, which is vast employment based on the inefficiencies of the system.

What is so horrifying about student anxiety is the way in which the administrative/bureaucratic apparatus of schools reacts to these statistics. Instead of auditing the system and understanding how the structure creates anxiety, and then deconstructing that system, and then reconstructing it so that the pressures are lessened, school districts simply create another bureaucratic response designed to signal. While it is certainly the case that there are students who need mental health supports that can only be offered through the school, it is hard to believe that with 96% of students reporting that "anxiety and depression" were either major or minor problems, that the school structure itself is not a major contributor.

Secondary students who have to manage the expectations of six different teachers and six different subjects, every day, might understandably develop anxiety. If those students are absent because of illness or a family death, they are all too often required to complete "make up work" on top of the physical or emotional trauma they have just suffered. The gears of the system just cannot stop grinding.

There seems to be no problem created by schools that can't be solved by a showpiece program. This creates confusion amongst students, many of whom are accused of being "snowflakes" in the popular media because they do not see either secondary schools or colleges as places to discuss and challenge ideas, but as places where an "everything is awesome here" message is perpetually flashing in neon.

The recent development of Chief Equity and Inclusion Officers, both at the K–12 level and at the university level, creates the impression that the bureaucratic structure is policing itself to eliminate racism, sexism, homophobia, etc. At first, this seems contradictory. School administration cannot advertise "we have a racism problem and are working to fix it." So, instead, they state "there is no racism, sexism, or homophobia here and here's the person who makes sure that is so." In other words, a set of speech codes are enforced by administration or through peer "cancellation" because any sense of controversy is bad for the brand of either the school district or the university.

This brings us to the most damaging analogy in modern education, and the guiding ideology of just about every institute of education in the country, that of "customer service." Secondary schools are places where everything is perfect and if parents complain, they must be appeased by administration. Under a customer service model of education, all of the bureaucratic structures are ultimately designed to deal with customer complaints.

Got a complaint about your mental health? Go to the mental health complaint department.

Got a complaint about systemic racism? Go to the equity and inclusion complaint department.

Got a complaint about sexual harassment or bullying? Go to the sexual harassment and bullying department.

None of these departments solve problems, although the people involved might be well-meaning and caring. The ultimate goal is to address the complaint, not the causes, and that renders the system inherently insincere. After all, the bells keep ringing, and the clientele keeps marching through the structure and by the time the clientele sees the inefficiencies, they will be out and another group of clients will be arriving.

The worst part of the structure is what it does to the people who succeed in it. In his condemnation of the Ivy League, *Excellent Sheep: The Miseducation of the American Elite and the Way to a Meaningful Life*, William Deresiewicz writes:

> What I saw at Yale I have continued to see at campuses around the country. Everybody looks extremely normal, and everybody looks the same. No hippies, no punks, no art school types or hipsters, no butch lesbians or gender queers, no black kids in dashikis. The geeks don't look that geeky; the fashionable kids go in for understated elegance. Everyone dresses as if they're ready to be interviewed at a moment's notice. (p. 21)

These are students who, from the time they enter an elite institution, are told they are the elite who made it through the intense winnow structure and they are now being educated as the future leaders in politics, finance, and academia. The system hyperinflates its own concept of a successful student, and, by proxy, no one says "we are reading the same books that are free at the library and listening to lectures that are inferior to what's on Youtube." That would seem to be contrary to the goals of the structure.

In a June 8, 2021, *Wall Street Journal* Op-Ed by R. R. Renoe, titled "Why I Stopped Hiring Ivy League Graduates," the author laments that students tend to become aggressive proponents of a liberalized mindset. Or "Normal kids at elite universities keep their heads down. Over the course of four years, this can become a subtle but real habit of obeisance, a condition of moral and spiritual surrender."

These young people are institutionalized. Stressed, normalized, depressed, anxious, and suppressed, these poor kids are the diamonds that the pressures of the structure create. And they then enter into the workplace with an inflated sense of self-worth, a need to pay off massive college debt, and a realization that they are of worth to the structure only through the signals that their successes help create for the next generation of young people who are moving through the institution. Any "success" achieved by an institutionalized individual entices others into it and upholds the structure. And the structure employs the bureaucracy.

Perhaps the most cynical act of modern education is the process of assigning grades. The process exists solely for the purpose of, to borrow Sanjay Sarma's word, "winnowing" students into categories based on their perceived performance. Ken Bain, author of *What the Best College Students Do* (2012) traced the history of the grade-giving process and stated:

> Somebody somewhere—probably at Oxford or Cambridge in the late 1700s—came up with a system of giving the best learners A's, the next B's, and so forth. It was just a system of shorthand that was supposed to describe how well people think. Through most of the 1800s, schools in England and the United States used only two grades. You either got credit for taking a course or you didn't. But by the late 1800s, schools had adopted a range of grades from A to F, from one to ten, or some other scale. In the twentieth century they added pluses or minuses. (p. 7)

Bain then notes that these grades tend to denote next to nothing about a student's actual abilities. From a rational perspective, the assignation of grades to a student is ridiculous on its face. Why stop at any stage in the learning process and issue a number or letter to where the student is at with her abilities? When people learn content and skills on their own, this is not part of the process. With almost any complex task, a beginner would get a grade of "F" at the start of the learning process. What good does it to codify that with a grade or letter?

Grades serve the purpose of the structure and are the means by which students are winnowed. The process of entering grades exhausts teachers, who must engage in this data-entry process along with planning lessons and actually delivering skills and content. (Indeed, the updating of the gradebook is often the only function that the bureaucracy cares about, because colleges, and therefore many parents, are interested in these grade point averages.) While grades may serve the purposes of the educational structure, they can create enormous and unnecessary damage to the psyches of young people.

A 2013 *Slate* article (https://slate.com/human-interest/2013/05/the-case-against-grades-they-lower-self-esteem-discourage-creativity-and-reinforce-the-class-divide.html) notes that poor educational outcomes in the United States could be linked to the use of the grading system. Among the dismal findings included in the article is "A 2002 study at the University of Michigan found that 80 percent of students surveyed based their self-worth on academic performance." The noted studies found that students with low self-esteem tend to have a low sense of self-worth, thus locking many students from poor communities into a cycle of "institutionalized" failure. Grades are a nonsensical system that allows a toxic sense of self to get absorbed directly into the bones of the most vulnerable students.

Some schools, although far too few, have broken away from the use of grades. Montessori schools are the most well-known but the author holds The Summerhill School in England up as an exemplar, where ". . . students are free to follow their own interests while teachers observe and nudge them toward new ways of thinking about what they're drawn to." This may sound hippie-drippy to educational reformers who would like to see the United States catch up to Taiwan in our science and math scores, but the concept of self-discovery is an important aspect of the educational process and remember, an MLM dispels the notion that learning that matters for one's life and career can only occur during one's youth. A student who fails to capture an interest in physics at age 15 need not fear that a physics teacher will only be available to her for a short period of time. Physics teachers are available on the internet, at all times, for free. (PBS crash-course physics is highly recommended.)

The reification of letter grades and scores as "things" that are inherent parts of a person's identity is inevitable. This brings us to our third point about the suburbs-to-college pipeline. This structure is dependent upon grading systems and it creates a systemic structure that, in turn, is exclusionary to individuals who are outside of it. In fact, since this pipeline corresponds generally with whiteness, one might see it as connected to issues of systemic racism.

Grades, GPAs, Intelligence Quotients, etc. eventually get absorbed as *objective* truths rather subjective measures. Stephen Jay Gould's skeptical masterpiece, *The Mismeasure of Man: The Definitive Refutation to the Argument of the Bell Curve* (1981) effectively made this case a long time ago, but the educational structure cannot winnow and select without the grading system, and the bureaucratic structure cannot be employed without it.

The supposed educational function of grades and scores is to develop a motivation in students that they did initially possess. Young people will not necessarily study just for the sake of learning, but must be put into an environment where the desire for "good" grades creates the pressure that creates the need. But educational motivation is a mystery beyond our understanding. Tara Westover, in her 2018 book *Educated: A Memoir* writes about how her father and mother moved the family out of society and provided virtually no formal education at all to their seven sons and daughters. Nonetheless, Tara studied independently and eventually earned a doctorate in intellectual history from Cambridge.

Tara's brother, Tyler, earned a Ph.D. from Purdue and gently disagrees with the overarching theme of Tara's book, something which he wrote in a blog. He noted that his father's animosity toward college education was not necessarily ill-founded. Young people who went to college rarely returned home to help with the problems in rural areas. Those of us in education should be careful when we say that education is a "way out" for students in impoverished areas; it should be a way to help.

Tyler's motivation to earn an engineering degree developed from the practical needs that he encountered while working, and his father's attempts to dissuade him from studying seemed to have the effect of making the young man develop an interest in learning. The fascinating case of the Westover family indicates that more research needs to be conducted into the motivational aspect of learning. Surely there are more effective ways to inculcate motivation than through the arbitrary pressure of grades.

An alternative to grades would be assessments for mastery purposes and this needs to be analyzed because tests have been co-opted by the educational industry. There is nothing wrong with the College Board Assessments such as the SAT or the Advanced Placement Exams in the way that those tests assess content and skills. The problem with Advanced Placement courses is that the College Board has developed an economic model based on the issuance of one test per year. The tests themselves are autopsies, a final assessment of a learning process that supposedly occurred during the school year. College Board rigorously scores the AP exams, including extensive writing portions, and then issues a score of 1–5. That score is the autopsy report.

Assessments that are issued in this way are not aligned with educational theory. Remember in the Introduction of this book where World Map Quiz was mentioned as an effective way to learn the geographic placement of countries on a map? World Map Quiz offers no tutorials and no learning mechanisms of any kind. It is purely an assessment that can be taken over and over and over again. If the quiz tells you to find Guatemala on the map and you click on Honduras, you will be told that you are wrong and the quiz then highlights where Guatemala is actually located. The next time that Guatemala is mentioned, you are more likely to click on the country immediately south of Mexico. Play the game a few dozen times and you will develop a basic understanding of world geography, play it a few hundred and you will likely develop a mastery, play it long enough and your thumbs will fly to the right countries. Play it once and you will likely just determine that you are "bad at geography."

In his 2021 book *How We Learn: The New Science of Education and the Brain*, Dehaene writes:

> If grades are hardly effective, then what is the best way to incorporate our scientific knowledge of error processing into our classrooms? The rules are simple. First, students must be encouraged to participate, to put forth responses, to actively generate hypotheses, however tentative; and second, they must quickly receive objective, non-punitive feedback that allows them to correct themselves.
>
> There is a strategy that meets all these criteria, and all teachers know about it: it is called . . . testing! What is less well-known is that dozens of scientific publications demonstrate its effectiveness. Regularly testing students' knowledge, a method referred to as "retrieval practice," is one of the most effective educational strategies. Regular testing maximizes long-term learning. The mere act of putting your memory to the test makes it stronger. It is a direct reflection of the principles of active engagement and error feedback. Taking a test forces you to face reality head-on, to strengthen what you know, and to realize what you don't know.
>
> The idea that testing is a cornerstone of the learning process is not self-evident. Most teachers and students see tests as a simple means of grading—their role is merely to assess the knowledge which has been acquired elsewhere, during class or while studying, Such ranking or grading, however, turns out to be the least interesting part of the test. What matters isn't the final grade that you get, but the effort that you make to retrieve information and the immediate feedback that you receive. (pp. 214–215)

This distills three simple rules: (1) Teach less. (2) Test a lot more. (3) Grade not at all.

Math students, for example, will often get tripped up when they see an equation like $x^2 = 49$. Most people with even a passing knowledge of mathematics will be able to see that the x must be 7 because $7 \times 7 = 49$. More important than the answer is the concept that one should take the square root of both sides. Putting x^2 under a discriminant has the effect of eliminating the 2 as an exponent. Putting 49 under the discriminant reduces it to 7.

Students who are constantly tested on this single concept might then see $x^2 = 9$. Putting x under the discriminant eliminates the exponent of 2 and putting the 9 under the discriminant reduces the 9 to 3. Answering 15 questions like that, and getting the first 10 wrong but the last 5 right would lead to a failing overall "grade." But what does that mean? Getting the last 5 right would indicate that the tester learned the skill after a process of trial and error. This is the difference between using testing as a method of teaching and using it as autopsy of the learning.

Isn't constant testing just a variation of what is done through textbook-and-workbook problems? When students in mathematics work through problems in the book and then look in the back for answers, isn't that the same?

No, not quite. The problem there is that students often see that kind of work, where the teacher assigns problems 10–30 for tomorrow, as arbitrary. Students who feel the pressure to achieve high grades will do the work, but many students view assignments like this as bewildering, something that causes stress if the parents are watching the gradebook, or becomes a source of downwardly spiraling self-esteem if the parents are not.

Another problem with duplicate worksheets, or even computer programs, is that they lend themselves to cheating. Cheating is the most cynical act that an alienated student can engage in. Cheating is when students see no value at all in the actual learning of content, but only see value in the social signal, or the release of outside pressure, that a "good grade" can bring.

This is just a suspicion of this author, but colleges and universities would seem to have little incentive to make a cheating scandal go public unless it was too egregious to ignore. At the K–12 level, students who copy and paste Wikipedia entries or who copy worksheet answers in the hallway from friends (or text each other answers) are not tracked by any internal system. Such cases are treated as individual violations of classroom or school codes, and generally dealt with as minor infractions. Only high-profile cases at elite institutions ever get reported to the media.

A 2007 scandal at Florida State involving tutors and online tests netted 61 school athletes, 25 of whom were football players. In 2012, 125 students in a government class at Harvard got busted for cheating on a take-home(!) exam. In May of 2021, 73 first-year cadets at West Point were accused of cheating on a calculus exam. Fifty-two of the accused were on the football team. In 1994, 134 students at the Naval Academy cheated on an electrical engineering exam, by buying a purloined copy of the test. In 2007, 50% of the students in a second-year dentistry program at Indiana University used an exam copy that had been hacked from the professors to help them cheat. These are just a few examples.

Surely, the number of cheating cases goes under-reported and none of these cases would include the much more pernicious and widespread cases of low-level learning. As early as 2010, Nichola G. Carr pointed out the problem in his book *The Shallows: What the Internet Is Doing to Our Brains*. Carr interviewed star students who had learned that they did not really need to read the books assigned to them because Wikipedia provided online summaries of ideas that provided enough information to construct a thesis statement and a paper. "Patchwriting" where students change the words slightly from previously published works is generally an efficient way to avoid plagiarism accusations. Students learn how to skim works and scam the system. If they don't, they get outcompeted for grades by students who can do this.

Fraternities offer social networks and recruit members by offering life-long business and social connections in politics and business. The fact that fraternity members are overwhelmingly white and economically well off, would seem to make them primary problems in the development of the exact kinds of exclusionary systems now decried by so many. Fraternities exist only because of the cynicism in the structure; they prize personal connections over actual learning. The cheating problem has always been at a crisis level in the Greek system, but institutions have little incentive to hold students accountable.

Fraternity involvement in cheating was shockingly revealed by the 2014 University of North Carolina scandal:

> University of North Carolina athletes weren't the only group benefiting from the college's recently exposed 18-year, 3,100-student cheating scandal—fraternity members did, too. More than 700 fraternity brothers, and some sorority sisters, took the no-attendance, no-professor, one-assignment "paper classes" that earned them easy A's and B's. Some fraternity members took so many African and Afro-American studies courses—the ones revealed to be rigged—that they accidentally earned minors in the subject.
>
> Discussion of fraternity members' enrollment in the irregular classes spans several paragraphs in the 136-page report containing the results of an eight-month *investigation* by former United States Department of Justice prosecutor Kenneth Wainstein. The findings, released Wednesday, exposed paper classes from 1993 to 2011 in which students could get high grades with little effort.
>
> "The largest source of referrals for non-athlete students—besides word-of-mouth—was the fraternity network on campus," the report reads. "One student . . . learned early on from his brothers about an AFAM administrator named Debby Crowder who was very accommodating. . . . [S]he would enroll him in a 'paper class,' which he understood to be an independent studies class for which one was guaranteed an A or A− simply for submitting a 10-page paper." (https://www.ibtimes.com/unc-cheating-scandal-hundreds-fraternity-brothers-took-paper-classes-boost-gpas-1711399)

A qualitative 1992 study by Donald McCabe and William Bowers found that 67% of students at 31 colleges and universities *self-reported* that they had cheated on classwork or exams. A replicated study that same year by Anna Williams and Steven M. Janosik found a number of 74%. Fraternities and sororities seem to incubate the problem by overwhelming members with social activities and opportunities while at the same time pressuring those students to retain high GPAs.

Altogether, these incidents and findings indicate that few college graduates made it through the system without either directly and knowingly cheating or at least engaging in the shallow "skim and scam" process of education. It's likely that huge numbers of collegians get through with a combination of both. How many individuals are now in powerful positions, partially based on their degree credentials, that never really received any education at all? The collegiate Greek system messages that only social connections are important for future success and athletic programs essentially turn students into full-time athletes. In either case, the student gets a clear message: "this content and these skills are not worth anything, just the signaling that comes from the appearance of having mastered them."

An ungenerous view of the education might bet that the skills that young people learn by just growing up in a suburban home, going to museums, and listening to NPR in the car are about the skill level that schools are designed to measure. It's a classic case of shooting the arrow into the barn and then painting the bulls eye around it.

How can all of this be fixed?

Chapter 5

The Mastery-Learning Model

A Mastery-Learning Model (MLM), also known as the Competency Model, is defined as one where a student must actually demonstrate the mastery of a skill set before moving on to another topic. Before the MLM can be fully understood, it must be compared to the Seat-Time Model (STM), also known as the Carnegie Model, that is typical for almost all K–12 and collegiate institutions. Embedded in the STM are several features that make learning difficult, and large-scale assessment of learning almost impossible, inefficient, and damaging to young people.

MLMs are effective. A 2005 study conducted in Turkey, published under the title of "The Effects of the Mastery-Learning Model on the Success of Students Who Attended a 'Usage of Basic Information Technologies' Course" was a study conducted on the premise where the researchers "... use a different approach to the instruction which does not place a premium on time in class." Importantly, all notions about group work were eliminated "The subjects, requiring individual practice are the ones where the students have the possibility to be alone and to practice by themselves."

The researchers included a section in their paper titled "How to Instruct for Mastery" and list several simple components, including, "clearly state the objectives representing the purposes of the course" and dividing the curriculum into subsections, each of which has its own objective and repeatable assessments. The purpose of the assessments is not to provide a learning autopsy for students, but to provide corrections for them as they continue toward mastery.

While the results of the pre-test that the researchers gave to the control group and the experimental group were similar, the results found that the MLM experimental group scored significantly higher, more than enough to reject the null hypothesis, on both the final raw score and the achievement component, which is measured by how much a student learned between the pre and post-test. The authors concluded that "There came to be strong reasons why instruction should abandon a standard like '70% is passing.' Such a statement means that some things have been learned and some have not, whereas the aim should be that all of the objectives of instruction are mastered."

Any reader of such common sense will immediately ask "why don't schools use the MLM then?" The purpose of explaining and excoriating the medieval STM in previous chapters was to answer that question. The STM with its grades and signals sustains a massive and ineffective bureaucracy. The MLM would eliminate that bureaucracy.

Several factors are likely to shift the current educational economic model, and with it, facilitate a change away from the destructive seat time conceit to a system of mastery learning. The 2020–2021 pandemic year forced many workplaces to develop a reliance on interfacing forms of technology, like Zoom or Google Meet, that allowed for meetings and discussions to take place virtually rather than in-person.

The effects of this on education have already been discussed here, but it is worth reiterating that the overall effect of virtual learning was to reveal the STM as absurd at every level of secondary and post-secondary education. As has been argued in this book, education cannot be divorced from larger social and economic trends. Two post-pandemic trends are likely to facilitate a shift toward the MLM: these are the disintegration of the suburbs, a societal intolerance for exclusivity, and collegiate and workplace movement toward the MLM.

At the same time that the pandemic was revealing the possibility of at-home work, internet broadband connections are spreading out into rural areas, allowing for cheap internet access away from congested urban and suburban centers. News stories about the trend, or at least the latent desire, to move to the country for the purpose of working remotely popped up regularly in 2021, but one survey will serve many. Two-thirds of Americans state that they would consider moving to the country if they work remotely, but of the 500 workers polled, one-third would need reliable internet service to make this possible (https://www.nextgov.com/cio-briefing/2020/10/remote-work-has-two-thirds-americans-considering-moving-cities-country/169598/).

Most notably, Silicon Valley tech companies have realized they don't actually need to be in Silicon Valley. Or, more metaphorically, they can move Silicon Valley to the "cloud" and avoid the expenses of actual meeting places. Property values will fall dramatically in suburban regions, and the ability to work remotely will likely entice a massive process of spreading out.

Rural schools, which have faced declining student populations for decades, cannot handle a massive influx of suburbanites. And, just as importantly, it's probably not the case that rural schools will be able to handle the sudden demands that working parents from the suburbs can place on educational institutions. If the suburban schools face a decline in student enrollment (an inevitability anyway, given the current baby bust), then school personnel will have to be cut back. This could be good news for rural communities that have long been suffering from brain-drains and economic droughts. There are few good reasons for businesses to move to rural areas, but if populations of remote workers start moving into the country, then the kinds of businesses that can thrive with that clientele will pop up to meet a new demand.

Second, as has been stated, the "winnowing" function of schools is designed around a seemingly obsolete concept of exclusivity. Although "Critical Race Theory" as an offshoot of the Black Lives Matter movement has become an educational strawman of sorts for many in the political-entertainment business, the concepts have filtered into education. The existence of Chief Equity Officers and the entire conceit of "equity" (giving students what they need to be equal as opposed to giving equal resources to students) is built upon the idea that inherent and race-based inequalities are built into American history and, consequently, into the American experience.

All of this is disputable, but also irrelevant. If it is true that the central story of American history is the development of inequity based on racism, then there are two ways to address this. The first is to create a new bureaucratic wing dedicated to sanitizing campuses of racism, restructuring curricula, and reeducating school personnel. The second is to create a core curricula that can be delivered, for free, to students anywhere and under any circumstances. Proponents of Critical Race Theory do need to be careful, however, of propagating the notion that America's structures are inherently inequitable or "rigged" against students of color. This is precisely the moment in American education when genuine equity can be delivered through MLMs. Students will need to believe that this system can work, and understand that their own motivation and discipline will lead to success.

With MIT offering a MicroMasters program under a Mastery-Learning Model, and employers starting to develop internal degree programs, a new vision of how the MLM could be adopted will be laid out here and this vision is compatible with current trends that seem solid moving into the future. Here's what education could look like.

An MLM operates through replicable online modules. The concept is that all of the materials necessary for learning content and skills are available, at all times, in these self-contained modules. Importantly, especially for mathematics education, is the fact that students can access how-to videos and watch them as many times as necessary. The supposed difficulty of mathematics and physics education is often a byproduct of students only seeing the teacher work through problems once or twice, while the students are in uncomfortable environments.

Students may need to see a problem and formula up to six or seven times, in addition to working practice problems, before really understanding the content and procedures. Easily accessible videos mean that students can watch a tutorial any number of times and pause and rewind easily to help assist in understanding. All of this can occur outside of an intimidating environment, and without potentially exhausting a teacher's patience.

Easily accessed examples of MLMs can be found through MIT's Micro-Masters program, or Harvard X. But www.physicsclassroom.com is sequential and impressive. For world history students www.patrickmanning.com provides a comprehensive world history education from one of the field's few genuine experts. The work need not be done all on the computer, as printable PDFs allow for a more traditional reading experience.

Most students experience some ineffective variation of an MLM either through online academies, charter schools, or through "credit recovery" programs (to be taken if a student fails an ordinary in-person class). This likely is what has created a reputation that MLMs are opposed to face-to-face instruction, or that they can only be offered as a secondary experience that is not as the traditional classroom. There need not be any false choice between MLMs and face-to-face learning.

To be clear; a modified version of MLM can solve most of the problems inherent in the STM, still provide the same resources for physical and mental health, and will do a better job of actually educating students. The development of the MLM will require some level of legislation or intervention from the U.S. Department of Education. Either (A) state governments can require that an MLM be offered in public schools as an alternative choice to the STM or (B) the federal government requires that the MLM be offered in public schools as an alternative to the STM as a condition of public funding.

Who will create the Mastery Learning Curriculum? This can be accomplished by centralized forces at the universities and, through a new conception of the teacher's role and of teacher professional development. So far, MLMs created by private tutoring services and through nonprofits tend to be the most effective. Students watching a video on YouTube want to get straight to the content and there need to be images and clear explanations. Simply taping a live lecture at a university is not as effective, since in-person education seems to require "get to know you" conversations between teachers and students. These are important for that environment but have no function at all in an online module.

The concept here is that from grades 7–12, students would go to school with a cohort of students. They will learn one subject at a time until mastery. What does this mean?

An MLM suits itself best to mathematics. Either students know how to complete quadratic equations, or they don't. Students can either apply trigonometric functions or they can't and this is demonstrable through an online module and can be developed through constant assessment. For geography, a game like World Map Quiz can be played repeatedly until the student demonstrates a mastery of the globe's geographic and physical features. But what about a subject as contentious as history?

The very existences of the 1619 Project and its counterpart, the 1776 Project indicate the current state of political animosity that is inherent in secondary history education. The only way to avoid being overwhelmed by controversy, as Project Based Learning (PBL) would have it, is to simply ask the students the question. A module for a U.S. history course that has standards from the colonial era to the Civil War might simply be:

What is the main narrative of U.S. history from the colonial era to the present?

Students could then engage with learning modules, even the 1619 and 1776 Projects, for the purpose of analyzing those approaches so that the questions could be answered. Modules might include themes such as:

- Seventeenth-century colonization and the interaction with Native Americans
- The Enlightenment and its effects on the American colonies and France
- The transatlantic slave trade
- The development of feminism

Each module would include readings, reading comprehension questions, and short videos. The purpose of the modules is to assist students in the process of answering the central question. Students can answer the question with a multimedia presentation or a traditional paper but must show evidence that they have mastered an understanding of the arguments.

Likewise, a world history course might require that students connect an understanding of geography with a general understanding of how history has shaped the current events of specific regions. The students could pick four or five key countries/regions, and study how those histories created the current economic and political situation.

It is neither hard nor expensive to create mastery learning modules like this and students can be tested so frequently that the mastery of the content through those tests will both assist them in their learning processes and completely eliminate the need for work to be graded.

In a structure like this, students could still go to school, but it would be possible to keep them with a core of other students (not that different from the typical elementary school) and students would only really need to engage with the modules for about 3 hr a day. Streamlining the educational process would reduce wasted time and allow students to focus only on the mastery of specific skills.

The second part of the day is where the school day could really be altered. Students might be able to engage in actual physical education in the sense that kids would walk, jog, play pick-up basketball, lift weights, or engage in other recreational activities. Can anyone find a good explanation for why, in the United States, school districts insist on fielding teams filled with the best athletes who then engage with each other in various forms of mock combat?

It is bizarre that educational institutions sport names like "Tigers" or "Marauders" or "Bobcats." The purpose of these nicknames always seems to be to showcase violence and aggression, with the mascots and emblems in a gym or on a field designed to intimidate incoming schools. No schools have "scholar," "feminists," or "environmentalists" as their mascots, although those nicknames would showcase the importance of intellectual work, gender equality, and cooperation.

Competitive sports could easily be replaced with physical activity. In his book *Exercised: Why Something We Never Evolved to Do Is Healthy and Rewarding* (2021), Daniel Lieberman wrote about his efforts to bring back physical education requirements at Yale that have been repeatedly denied. Yale provides students with a full course of intercollegiate athletic programs, however, thus promoting the now-prevalent idea that exercise is primarily for elite athletes.

Other options for the second half of the day might include letting the older students get jobs. Working at a fast food restaurant and having to fill orders during a dinner-time rush will certainly give young people a quick education in teamwork, cooperation, and work ethic. It might also help to prevent some of the psychological and emotional effects, so prevalent among students who show promise at an early age, that being told about one's "elite" status can bring.

There seems to be strong evidence that teens want to work. In the summer of 2021, teens were instrumental in filling service sector jobs that would otherwise have suffered from labor shortages. In June of that year, one-third of 16- to 19-year-olds were working. Getting an actual job might be the antidote to the epidemic of young people feeling pressure to build up a "well-rounded" college application by engaging perpetually in nonprofit work, mission trips, and extracurriculars.

An MLM is, by necessity, individualistic in nature and this is reflective of reality. Knowledge and cognitive skills can only be developed through individual practice; the brain is naturally sociable but does not naturally calculate derivatives or write essays on Greek literature. But just because the process of acquiring knowledge and skills must be done individually, this does not mean that a process of intellectual networking cannot occur as part of the MLM experience. Indeed, the problem with "group projects" as traditionally developed in classrooms, is that they are not aligned with what MIT data scientist Alex Pentland calls "social physics."

In his book, *Social Physics: How Social Networks Can Make Us Smarter* (2014), Pentland defines the title phrase:

> Social physics is a quantitative social science that describes reliable, mathematical connections between information and idea flow on the one hand and people's behavior on the other. Social physics helps us understand how ideas flow from person to person through the mechanism of social learning and how this flow of ideas ends up shaping the norms, productivity, and creative output of our companies, cities, and societies. It enables us to predict the productivity of small groups, of departments within companies, and even of entire cities. It also helps us run communication networks so that we can reliably make better decisions and become more productive. (p. 4)

Pentland wrote an entire book on the concept and how it can be used to make conversations educationally productive, so his findings are too exhaustive to be fully recounted here. It is enough to say that with social physics as a guide, truly effective forms of communication between students can be established. Instead of having students engage in group discussions based on arbitrary criteria, for the last 10 minutes of class, students could be grouped together based on their shared interests.

Additionally, and this may sound surprising, there really is no compelling need to require that students show mastery of writing in an MLM module. This is because a person's level of reading comprehension, which is more testable, almost directly connects with a person's writing ability. (Anecdotally, has there ever been a talented writer who did not first develop by voraciously reading?)

Writing, like other creative activities, might be better suited to afternoon club work. Master of Fine Arts (MFA) programs that are featured in some universities, most famously at the University of Iowa, offer an applicable model for how students might discuss each other's creative work. The same concept could be applied to ethics, artistic creations, robotics, etc. Teachers can benefit from significant research that has been conducted on the topic of conversations, but most importantly a cultural shift must occur. School is where we learn how to think and talk about controversial issues, not where we avoid them.

What would the role of the teacher be in a school based on the MLM? As of now, public school teachers are responsible for planning lessons for each day, often for multiple subjects, for monitoring student progress, recording grades, and often coaching sports or sponsoring other extracurriculars as well. This is in addition to attending meetings and fulfilling obligations required by state and district bureaucracies; the scale of the workload becomes overwhelming.

A new concept of teaching and what it means to engage in professional development has been the focus of my research. In 2012, *Skeptic* magazine published a paper of mine called *Three Cheers for Teachers: Education Reform Should Come From Within the Classroom and Science Can Inform Those Reforms*. To summarize that essay: "teaching" should be redefined as a field in itself, separate from Education (which is research-based). Teaching as a field would involve the teacher (A) learning new content and (B) synthesizing that content with educational methods to create (C) a Teacher-Generated-Curriculum (TGC) that combines content area knowledge with actual learning theory in a way that textbooks and workbooks do not. The TGC is the equivalent, for the field of teaching, of what a research-based paper would be for education or some other research-based field.

That conception, which grew out of my doctoral work, became the guiding philosophy for a series of summer institutes which were funded with a combination of funding from the Indianapolis-based Scientech Foundation and the state of Indiana. The concept behind the institute has a deep research base but can be described fundamentally as connecting teachers to professors in the content fields and also with local businesses and nonprofits.

The set-up for the Institutes was simple; teachers either learned content from professors in math, physics, chemistry, or biology for 2 hr or the teachers worked with local businesses and nonprofits for 2 hr. Then, for the next 2 hr they worked together, alone, or with educational methods specialists to synthesize that content with best practices in educational methodology. The result, for each teacher, was a classroom-ready TGC.

The objective of the summer institute was to make professional development like a greenhouse; in the same way that a greenhouse creates the right conditions for plants to grow, the summer institutes created the right conditions for ideas to grow. Effective educational leadership tends to be the creation of the right conditions for teachers to recognize their visions, not for pre-ordained experts to pressure teachers into adopting the vision of an administrator or "expert."

Often the effective TGC delivers content to students in innovative and engaging ways, at least partially through high-level reading, and then assesses students by having those students apply their knowledge to a novel situation. In law, medicine, and the sciences the point of learning *old* information is to apply that knowledge for the analysis of a *new* situation. In law, this involves the use of precedent, in medicine it is necessary for diagnostics.

The role of the teacher in MLM would be to act as the "expert in the room" to help students when they have questions. In addition, each MLM would have a built-in gap that would allow for teachers to implement curriculum that is specifically tailored to the needs of the local community. This would address Tyler Westover's concern (mentioned previously) that, in many rural or urban areas where there is poverty and high need, it seems to be the case that education has the effect of sending people away.

Under this type of system, teachers would be seen more as professionals who develop and shape their field, rather than as employees who implement the vision of administration. Teachers would not have to make daily "lesson plans" or grade papers. Instead, they would spend time connected to the business and college community and would develop high-level curricula. With this model, fewer teachers could facilitate larger numbers of students, and students would not need to be shuffled arbitrarily from class to class. Instead, students could stay with an initial cadre of students (and why not celebrate Halloween and birthdays in these cadres, or play some Scrabble every now and then?) and seek out teachers as the need arises.

The MLM would prepare students for their next phases in life. If universities began to shift toward lending their prestige to the mastery of skills, there is no reason that someone from an impoverished community could not get a job at Best Buy while also developing his skills as a mechanical engineer. Obviously, at some level, students who want to enter medicine or into advanced chemistry or physics would need to enter graduate schools, and face-to-face education will always be crucial, but the costs of undergraduate education no longer need be incurred, and students no longer need to suffer from the failures of the STM.

Chapter 6

Why Education Is Sequestered From Economic Trends and Innovation and How to Change This

The tech and financial sectors of society continue to be transformed by the rapid one-to-one transmissions allowed by cellphones and satellite connectivity. Just a few decades ago, banks operated by holding money in their vaults, and then lending it out with interest to borrowers. People put their wealth in banks for two reasons: (1) Protection of their assets, especially after the Franklin-Roosevelt-era FDIC insurance protections. (2) The bank pays a modest rate of interest to people who put their savings into the bank.

But, as Daniel P. Simon put it in his book *The Money Hackers: How a Group of Misfits Took on Wall Street and Changed Finance Forever*, cell phone technology makes a new kind of lending possible, one that allows for individuals rather than banks to leverage for a maximum return on their money. Simon uses two fictional characters, Charlie and Joe, to make his point:

The idea of peer-to-peer lending is simple:

What if Charlie just lent money directly to Joe?

If borrowers and investors could bypass the banks, then that would mean none of their money would go toward paying for the bank and its infrastructure. By cutting out the middle man, Charlie can offer a loan to Joe at a lower rate than the bank could have offered, and he can make a higher return on his investment than he would have made if he had kept a savings account at the bank. Both of them are getting a better deal if they cut out the middleman. (p. 20)

The vision quickly becomes apparent; computer programmers need to create user transactions where the interest rate on a loan goes down while the interest rate on the investment goes up. What allows for this magic is the elimination of all the hierarchical structure that comes from a brick-and-mortar bank. Tellers, managers, secretaries, and guards are as obsolete as the 1930s bank robbery.

The challenge for peer-to-peer lending was in the development of supervisory measures where lenders and borrowers would feel that their money was protected. During the 2020 pandemic, when many schools and universities were forced to adopt online learning, the concept of teacher-to-student learning, similar to peer-to-peer lending, surely occurred to millions of people. If teachers and professors could just deliver content and skills directly to students over zoom sessions, then parents or students could just pay teachers or professors directly. The costly "administrative" expenses associated with running campuses could be bypassed entirely.

The 2020–2021 pandemic shutdowns might have inaugurated the single largest embezzlement scheme in all of world history. Embezzlement occurs when a charge is collected for a service that was not actually rendered. While teachers and professors were required to continue courses over zoom sessions, school administrators collected their paychecks for no clear reason. If the circumstances warranted, as they seemed to in every school district across the country, that teachers be "held harmless" on their evaluations then administrators could forgo the evaluative processes that are supposed to be their main function.

If the administrative component of universities and public schools can be seen as directly analogous to their counterparts in banking, then there would seem to be a way to directly connect education to users in the same way that money can be transferred in peer-to-peer lending. The difference in the analogy is that the physical presence of a bank does not confer the same importance to society as the physical presence of a school.

This difference, plus archaic federal and state laws that mandate a seat-time model, is what sequesters the medieval bureaucracy of education from market forces. Consider this quote from Simon regarding how banks were outmaneuvered by online providers of secure money exchanges that were equipped to take advantage of smartphones:

> Shopping and sending money with our phones has become commonplace. This change didn't happen because of banks, though banks had all the technology they needed to do it. It happened because a few people outside of the banking industry saw what the banks weren't seeing, and they seized the opportunity.
>
> But banks see it now.
>
> In 2016, a consortium of some of the biggest banks in the United States—JPMorgan Chase, Bank of America, Wells Fargo, PNC, and others—formed a joint venture called Early Warning Services. The following year, the company released Zelle, a mobile app that lets users send money to other Zelle users—directly competing with Venmo [an online money-moving app].
>
> And because Zelle is operated directly by the banks, it is able to move the money instantly, without Venmo's one-to-three-day delay. (p. 13)

What we can see here is that the entirety of banking management, an unthinkably expensive clump of briefcases, suits, and MBA degrees, got outmaneuvered by a handful of computer programmers who, themselves, were just clever enough to predict that a lot of people would have cell-phones and would want to use them as a way to spend money.

Then, when the banking big-wigs assembled, all they could think to do was to copy the concept (and presumably kick the actual creating of the programs down to underpaid computer programmers) and then leverage the legal privileges that had been carefully built up by decades of lobbying, to provide a slightly faster turnaround rate than the "rogue" online money exchangers.

Interestingly enough, the way to make big money in the modern economy seems not to be in coding or programming, skills which seem ubiquitous in large segments of the population, but in the ability to find a way to fill a gap or eliminate costly "middlemen" in any form of transaction. Ultimately, the goal seems to be to eradicate archaic laws and bureaucracies so that an algorithm can automatically make the most beneficial transaction for the user.

In the past, large wealth-management firms invested money for investors, but because those firms kept a percentage cut of the money they helped to make from investments, it only made sense for those firms to take on high-dollar clients. As long as a wealth-management firm outperformed the relatively modest average rate of return (around 2%) provided by the market, then investors considered the cost to be worth it. But numerous studies show that wealth management firms do not outperform random investment choices. The big-money returns that big-money spenders enjoy were a result of diversification.

The stock market can be understood as a mismanaged casino. Casinos make money because the odds, in the aggregate, always favor the house. The only real way for an individual to make money in a casino is to hope to gain wealth on a single play. If a gambler has $1,000 to spend, the best option that the odds offer is to go straight to the roulette wheel and place all $1,000 either on red, black, odd, or even. Such a bet offers about a 45% chance (remember that double zeroes and the green are on the table) of doubling the gambler's money. If the gambler bets red and wins, then he should walk out of the casino. The odds will always favor the house in the long term, and the odds are more favorable to the house in frequent-play games like slot machines.

The stock market typically supplies about a 2% return to investors, which means that placing a single big bet, while potentially enriching, is a less good investment. Diversifying investments in various companies, unlike putting money into a variety of slot machines or onto different gambling tables, will almost always pay better for investors. Of course, only people with a lot of money can actually spread a lot of money around to different companies and so this makes it appear as if the wealth-management companies are doing something special to outperform the market.

In reality, anyone with a working knowledge of the market could do just about as well by investing a lot of money in low-risk stocks that will continually return on the investments. If casinos operated on the same principles as the stock market, then gamblers would be better off by spreading their money out into different games throughout the casino. This would be a quick way to lose a fortune in a real casino, but it works in the stock market.

What this shows is that the executives in wealth-management firms and the executives in top banking firms really are not doing anything useful at all. The same process seems to be occurring in higher education. The best (worst?) example comes from the University of Southern California where USC offered a $115,000 master's degree in counseling (https://www.wsj.com/articles/usc-online-social-work-masters-11636435900). USC's administration took the concept of the online learning modules, leveraged their power to bestow credentials, and then maximized their profit margin by cutting out brick-and-mortar costs but still charging brick-and-mortar rates.

USC's abuse of power is all the more egregious because counseling is such an essential role in mental health, and because many of the counselors in the program seemed to enter with only vague notions about how a USC graduate degree might help their careers (the answer being: not much). Sometimes good people are too trusting of others. Universities, in their quest for "diversity," have merely defined the term to be as financially beneficial for the schools as possible. If the government was handing out education grants, then it made sense for universities to accept as many applicants as possible and if government loans went out to minority students this looked all the better for public relations since it created the appearance that the universities were offering a path to societal equity. If students defaulted on loans, the universities did not suffer at all, because the schools did not have to pay the money back.

K–12 school districts, colleges, and universities are all behaving the same way as the big banks; devoid of ideas and outmaneuvered by programmers in the private market, they collapse back onto their legally given ability to hand out credentials. The educational economic model is built upon the fact that schools can verify a person's educational attainment and this takes priority over a school's ability to deliver the skills and content.

But verifiability of skills is precisely what a blockchain, the same kinds that verify the history of economic transactions, can provide for education. Of blockchains, Simon writes:

> Blockchain, the technology that makes bitcoin possible, allowed for the creation of a new decentralized form of money. But what if money was just the beginning?

What if blockchain was also capable of decentralizing other functions of our society, removing the need for intermediaries and "trusted third parties" up and down many sectors? What if, in addition to being used to record the transfer of bitcoin, the blockchain were used to record the transfer of stocks, real estate deeds, and any other asset?

Blockchain is a ledger that can be updated securely and instantly, and it's immutable: once it's updated, it can't be tampered with. What if it were used to record votes? What if a blockchain could be used to replace or improve *every* transaction that depends on a trusted third party? (p. 150)

In the case of education, the third party is school administration. The teacher and the student are the other two parties; the teacher passes education and skills on to a student, but the third party administrative apparatus must verify the transaction. YouTube, libraries, and online learning modules have collapsed the price of education for learning's sake to nearly nothing, but the third-party verification of the transactions is what schools can now charge a high premium for.

The immediate objection to such a notion is that the face-to-face interactions that in-person schools offer are worth an extra cost. This point is not debatable, and nowhere in this book will it be argued that students should not have the opportunity to physically attend school. But it is now possible to envision a future of education where students could spend a substantial portion of their time in school working on Mastery Learning Modules. Grades and grading would be unnecessary in such a structure because students could study and test until mastery, and then have their mastery verified by the blockchain, thus adding a credit to what we will call an educational record (ER).

The ER could, in turn, potentially streamline the college admissions process. The current process is absurdly subjective, inequitable, inefficient, stress-inducing, and ruinously expensive. Each school district keeps records of students and those records, along with contrived essays and teacher letters of recommendation are part of a package sent by students to admissions offices. There is no way that a structure like this can provide equity to underserved populations of students because the ability to recognize the structure and then meet the needs of the application rubric is beyond most teenagers and requires adult navigation.

In finance, any use of a "middleman" agent, or any bureaucratic interruption in a financial transaction, is referred to as a "pain point." The eventual goal of computer programmers is to reduce the pain point to an unthinking immediate reaction on the part of an algorithm that maximizes the benefit of the user with almost no thought process. So, for example, an app on someone's phone could read the trends of the market and authorize a trade, or round up a transaction (as the app Acorn does) so that the extra money gets placed into the stock market automatically on the behalf of the user.

A blockchain for education could create an ER on behalf of each student and this could operate as educational currency in the same way that Bitcoin does. Bitcoin has a built-in regulatory system that works as such: Bitcoin is "mined" by having computers solve mathematical problems; the solutions to those problems are verified by other computer programs. Because the earliest problems are the easiest to solve, meaning they require less computational capacity, Bitcoin was easy to create in the beginning. However, as the problems have gotten more complex, Bitcoin has become harder to mine and requires more computational power; this means that Bitcoin's value has tended to inflate as time has gone by, making the value of the early Bitcoin (considered close to worthless even by early adopters) suddenly rise.

At first glance, Bitcoin would seem to be an extension of pointless bureaucratic labor. The mathematical problems that are solved seem to have no actual value to anyone, and the value of cryptocurrency is purely subjective (hence its well-known volatility) but a discussion of Bitcoin and its derivatives is not the subject here. Bitcoin can provide a model for a new educational admissions process.

Students working within a Mastery-Learning Model can simply "mine" credit by mastering skills and the value of mastery could be assigned similarly to that of Bitcoin. For example, mastering basic arithmetic could be worth one point, algebra could be worth two points, algebra II three points, geometry four points, and calculus five points. Three points total might need to be earned for a high school diploma, but a student may need to earn fifteen points total in order to enter college that focuses on mathematics and engineering.

For students, their credits would just accrue upon "levelling up" on their education, and they could use their credits to buy admission to the campus of their choice. The admissions process would be unnecessary because a certain level of accumulated points in various subjects would be the only criteria for entrance. When one considers that the primary function of a guidance department at both the secondary and collegiate level is to guide students through their necessary graduate requirements, a simple points-based system like this could direct students easily through the structure. Guidance counselors could then focus on student mental health and also try to connect students with community partners and job opportunities.

Discussions on education tend to be self-contained; defenders of the SAT and ACT, for example, note that success on those exams tends to equate to success in college. That may be true, but does success in college translate to doing something useful in society? In the modern, bureaucracy-chocked capitalist economy, a high level of education has a tendency to remove a person from meaningful work. Capitalist theorists should pay close attention to the following case.

In Eau Claire, Wisconsin, in the Eau Claire school district, where a substitute-teacher shortage threatened to shut down schools in late 2021, the superintendent worked as a substitute teacher for a couple of half-days (https://www.weau.com/2021/12/20/ecasd-administrative-staff-stepping-ease-substitute-teacher-shortage/). While this was likely a publicity stunt to try and entice people in the community to apply for substitute teaching jobs, it creates an interesting question: Why is it not the case that substitute teachers are having to fill in for a superintendent shortage?

If highly paid administrators can opt out of their meetings and bureaucratic make-work for even a few half-days then that means that they could probably opt out of those meetings every day. If the administration begins working as substitute teachers, then that means that the market is actually supporting a going rate for substitute teachers at an administrator pay rate.

Left to an open market, virtually any job will eventually attract applicants if the salary and benefits reach a high enough level. In schools, when that does not happen, salaried staff have to step in to fill the essential roles and that reveals the real worth of the work. If a school administrator can leave his ordinary job and substitute teach, then that means that his ordinary job is worth close to nothing in real value while substitute teaching is worth what the administrator is actually paid.

The logic here is manifestly obvious enough that most administrators will not actually chip in to help during a time of crisis. Teachers, instead, end up giving up prep periods or (very common at the elementary level) doubling up classes while administrators sit in meetings. That inequitable system is held together purely by an ideology that holds a hierarchical class to be superior in its own labor to the meaningful work done by teachers. Any time a hierarch engages in meaningful work, that reveals the true value of the labor and this becomes dangerous to the edifice.

Carmel Community Schools in Carmel, Indiana, is in one of the wealthiest suburbs in the United States and the district contains some of the finest facilities for promoting athletic and artistic achievements of any school district in the world. Carmel has one high school of over 5,000 students and that population size allows for Carmel to pick elite athletes and performers for competitions. The result is that Carmel High School has more state championships (the high school swim team is especially dominant) than any other high school in the United States.

Yet, the Carmel school district cannot get students to school effectively because of a bus driver shortage. Carmel is a high-profile community, regularly ranking in magazine-and-website surveys as one of the best places (sometimes *the* best) to live in the United States, and Carmel's bus driver woes continually upset the community. School district administration even offered a significant pay increase to classroom teachers if they would drive buses before and after school. When this failed to address the shortage, the administration was forced to triple-route the bus pick-ups, essentially tripling the workload on their existing drivers, in order to get students picked up and brought to school (https://youarecurrent.com/2021/08/11/nearly-1700-carmel-students-lose-bus-service-because-of-driver-shortage/).

This strange situation not only showcases the problems of school districts that are top-heavy with extracurricular fluff, but it also creates an interesting thought experiment. What if the five dozen or so Carmel administrators, most of whom enjoy full benefits packages and six-figure salaries, gave up their meetings, stopped engaging in teacher evaluations, and did not stand around doing lunch duty? What if they drove buses instead?

Would the students and parents in Carmel Community Schools notice that the administrative meetings were not attended, that the teacher evaluations were not complete, and that less people were standing around in the lunchrooms? Or would the parents and students just be happy to have a more efficient busing system?

In this regard, schools suffer from the same type of workplace crisis that seems to be affecting much of modern capitalist society. A high level of education all too often ushers people into jobs that lack meaning and have little or no actual purpose. Meanwhile, jobs with an actual purpose such as truck driving, food service, teaching, childcare, and construction work are suffering from shortages.

It turns out that a bureaucratic educational structure has the effect of churning out graduates that are prepared for bureaucratic jobs. This has created a situation where college graduates, carrying a combined $1.7 trillion in debt, are working in jobs without purpose while the less-educated working class is often making nice salaries working at jobs that have an essential purpose. K–12 and university education only avoid this overturning of the economy because state legislators fund educational institutions with lump-sum payments, and the administrative class, rather than an open market, dictates how the money is allocated.

The reason that this education-to-bureaucracy pipeline is ignored, according to anthropologist David Graeber, is because the reigning economic theories deny that the phenomenon can exist. The capitalist conceit is that businesses in a free market must compete with each other and so this causes them to filter out meaningless bureaucracy so that profits can be maximized. The competition itself forces out waste. A capitalist economy differs from a command economy in this way because in Communist-controlled economies, the desire of the Party to boast full employment leads to the creation of pretend jobs and waste.

Graeber created the term "Bullshit Jobs" for a 2013 article, and reprinted it in his book *Bullshit Jobs: A Theory* (2018); he noted that the 20th century saw reductions in actual "labor" based jobs such as maids, industrial workers, and farm-hands, but "At the same time, 'professional, managerial, clerical, sales, and service workers' tripled, growing 'from one-quarter to three-quarters of total employment.' In other words, productive jobs have, just as predicted, largely been automated away" (xvii).

A "Bullshit Job" has a specific meaning; Graeber defined it as a job so pointless that not even the person doing the job could justify its existence. Jobs such as this are not supposed to exist in capitalist economies, but their prevalence seems to indicate that the managerial class has created these jobs so that the managers have someone to manage. With so much money flowing through companies, the managerial class has learned to judge prestige, in part, by the number of people that a manager has "under" him.

Someone with a job as a "duct taper," according to Graeber, fixes a problem that need not exist in the first place if the organization was running more smoothly. If there is a bump in the floor, for example, a duct taper would stand by the bump to grab people as they tripped. If the bump was smoothed out, then the duct taper's job would no longer exist. "Box tickers" are individuals who get paid to appear as if they are busy. "The most miserable thing," Graeber writes "about box-ticking jobs is that the employee is usually aware that not only does the box-ticking exercise do nothing toward accomplishing its ostensible purpose, it actually undermines it, since it diverts time and resources away from the purpose itself" (p. 45).

In his book, Graeber states higher education is bloated with Bullshit Jobs because it is unsightly for upper-level administrators to make too much money (they aren't football coaches after all!) and so the excessive amounts of money brought into universities through government education loans and the economic delusions that the baby-boomers held about their children ended up getting spent on the creation of useless middle-management positions.

It might be better, and certainly would be more politically correct, to call a Bullshit Job a seat-time job. A seat-time job is one where a person is supposed to fill a seat for a certain amount of time, and if the job requires very little in the form of actual labor, then the job-holder is expected to look busy. This seems very similar to what students are required to do in the Seat-Time Model of education; the educational structure then prepares students for wasteful jobs in the "real world."

According to Graeber, this has created a strange kind of economic calculus in capitalist economies as "purpose" of labor now has a kind of currency. Managerial jobs pay well, but the labor often seems to have no effect on anything. Trash collectors and teachers, however, supposedly get to see the direct and positive effects of their labor and that is supposed to take the form of actual monetary payments. In her book, *Work Won't Love You Back: How Devotion to Our Jobs Keeps Us Exploited, Exhausted, and Alone*, Sarah Jaffe writes that jobs in people-centric industries, such as nursing or elementary school teaching, come with pressure to "love" work that is often exhausting and demeaning. The love is almost never returned, however, by corporate managers who tend to see workers in these industries as replaceable.

Neither Graeber nor Jaffe writes about this, but there are interesting economic models that expand upon their points. In modern Western society, there still seems to be a value in engaging in meaningful artistic work. A 2014 blog entry by author and teacher John Warner warns writers who enter a master's in fine arts program for creative writing against believing that the degree will prepare them for a job in academia. He wrote that MFA programs graduate thousands of students every year but that, in 2014, a grand total of about 42 creative writing positions (that includes fiction, poetry, and creative nonfiction) were open, all of which will go to well-established and probably prize-winning authors (https://www.insidehighered.com/blogs/just-visiting/potential-mfa-students-there-are-no-academic-jobs).

The MFA in creative writing might be seen, therefore, as an economic model where people pay to engage in creative work that is seen to be meaningful by the artist. Obviously, people can write for free but if the only audience is literary agents who send form rejection letters, if that, then the work comes to feel just like any other type of labor that goes unrecognized in the work-for-pay world. The MFA program provides the writer with an audience, and with feedback from other people trying to engage in meaningful work but there is almost no economic payoff for the programs for graduates.

Still, based on the sentiments in Warner's blog entry, and from other online offerings by MFA teachers, a considerable number of students still pay to enter MFA programs in the hopes that the degree will eventually earn success in publishing and an academic career in writing. The desire to earn a living engaging in artistic or creative work seems to be strong enough to overwhelm economic realism for most of these students.

In this sense, the book-and-journal publishing industry is an interesting model because the actual articulation of ideas through writing seems to be worth almost nothing on the open market. Very few academic or science journals actually pay their writers anything at all and authors for academic presses usually receive only about 10 or 11% on their royalties. Only a very small number of writers will ever see a meaningful royalty from either a book of nonfiction or fiction.

This kind of market exists for two reasons. The first is that, in publishing, the editing, printing, and marketing of papers and books is expensive work, and the publisher assumes the financial risk. In the case of publishing, to cut out the "middleman" between the author and reader would be easy enough as authors can publish directly on webpages or through Amazon's e-publishing service. The problem is that editing is actually meaningful work, to be done in collaboration with authors, and that the services provided by book publishers do tend to guarantee that "published" books are written by experts in the field, have had some copy editing and peer-review, and are of a quality worthy of informed readers. In this model, the royalty paid to authors is not so much a means of income as a currency of legitimacy. The royalty the publisher pays to the author is a way of legitimizing an author's contribution more than it is a source of income.

The second reason such a market exists is that books, which pay little, and academic paper writing, which often pays nothing, have the effect of enhancing the prestige of the author. For professors in academia, or for scientists begging for research funding, publication is proof that an intellectual contribution has been made to society. Sometimes, this equates to a monetary value as is the case when big-name nonfiction authors, e.g., Malcolm Gladwell or Ibram X. Kendi, can charge high fees for speaking at events. In other cases, the publication can help a professor attain tenure or help an aspiring creative writing teacher to build up a *curriculum vitae*.

What the existence of the MFA, and book publishing in general, reveal is that a market exists to assist people in the creation of meaningful work. The acts of writing, painting, or pursuing an interest are all forms of labor. However, as Graeber noted, "work" has come to be defined as paying people to engage in labor that the worker does not want to engage in. And, as Jaffe states, the truly toxic add-on to that, for people who work in childcare or eldercare, is the pressure that workers feel to love their job. (Anecdotally, when teachers complain about the job in private or public, they tend to separate their love of kids from their distaste for the bureaucratic and political aspects of the job.)

"Meaningful work" might be defined as work that has its own inherent worth, even if that worth is simply in giving pleasure to the person who is engaged with it. People regularly pay to build with LEGOS, even though at some level that could be considered work, just as painting, writing, gardening, and exercise can. Each of those activities ends with the creation of a product and in each case the act of the labor itself tends to give pleasure to the person engaged with it. "Work," as Graeber states, is when a hierarch decrees a use for a subordinate's time. The underlying philosophy of the workplace, according to Graeber, is that when the employer buys time then the employer can direct that time, and since enjoyable work is not work at all, then "work" is defined as drudgery and if there is not enough work, then the employee is forced to pretend to work.

In Graeber's theory, capitalism and communism both create make-work jobs: capitalism to uphold the prestige of phony managers and communism to build in 100% employment and inflated numbers for gross domestic product. This theory would seem to run counter to traditional economic analysis, except for the fact that a study of history (and this goes beyond Graeber's book) seems to uphold the claim.

Capitalist historians and political analysts tend to equate "communism" with two forms of economic exploitation. The first involves the nationalization of private firms, such as occurred when Arbenz took over the United Fruit Company in Guatemala or when Chavez and Maduro nationalized (in a weird way, as a proxy to Cuba) the oil and natural gas industries in Venezuela. Nationalization of private corporations tends to put incompetent party bureaucrats in charge of a process they neither understand nor care to understand, and so nationalization usually destroys innovation, morale, and the economic structure that nurtured the private industry, to begin with.

The most dramatic example of a Communist bureaucratic interference came when the "Chief Designer" of the Soviet Rocket program, Sergei Korolev (1907–1966) died just as the Americans took control of the space race. The reason why the Americans took control after Korolev's death is because President John F. Kennedy, in 1961, had set the arbitrary goal of putting astronauts on the moon by the end of that decade.

The fact that Kennedy made his proclamation as a delayed American response to the launching of the Soviet satellite Sputnik in 1957 is an overdone part of the space race narrative. Neither Kennedy, his cabinet, nor anyone in the Soviet politburo likely had any idea what effect that Kennedy's goal really would have on the space race itself. In very simple physics terms: Kennedy was saying that the United States could put a heavier rocket on the moon than the Soviets could.

Adding three astronauts to a rocket meant adding life-sustaining equipment, and therefore weight. If Kennedy had stated, in 1961, that he wanted to put a tank, instead of three men, on the moon by the end of the decade then the effect would have been the same. The extra weight of the rocket meant that the oxygenated kerosene which had fueled the Soviet rockets could not create enough propulsion off the Earth's surface to reach escape velocity. Korolev understood this, but the Soviet bureaucrats did not. After the Chief Designer's death, the Soviet bureaucrats kept ordering that the 1950s Russian rocket designs just continually be scaled up. Kerosene fuel could provide liftoff for smaller rockets, but at a larger scale rattled them apart on the launch pad.

Meanwhile, the American space program, led by the American-captured Nazi Wernher von Braun (1912–1977) moved on to liquid hydrogen. Liquid hydrogen created a greater initial thrust which, in turn, allowed for the American rockets to push a greater payload off the surface of the Earth and to reach escape velocity. Liquid hydrogen is unsafe for a number of reasons, and in the modern era as private companies have looked to create private forms of space exploration, kerosene is still more effective at launching and controlling smaller rockets.

The Space X rockets, for example, are considerably smaller than the Saturn V rockets that NASA used in the moon landings of the 60s and 70s (https://provscons.com/heres-why-spacex-uses-kerosene/) and for a number of reasons involving safety and cost, Space X has chosen to use kerosene as the primary fuel.

It has taken about five decades for private industry to figure out what Korolev knew upon his death in 1966. Kerosene is the most effective fuel for smaller rockets, and there are only arbitrary reasons to make bigger rockets. If we consider the NASA spaceflight program, as we should, as a component of the U.S. nuclear weapons program then the entire package could be rolled into a single make-work form of a command economy. In his masterful book, *Command and Control: Nuclear Weapons, the Damascus Incident and the Illusion of Control* (2013) and the equally impressive documentary made about the book, Eric Schlosser noted that in the early days of the Cold War, the men in the nuclear program estimated that about one or two hundred nuclear weapons would be enough to obliterate the Soviet Union.

Yet, the United States ended up building about 30,000 nuclear weapons. National Security can hardly be stated as the reason for the build-up, as Schlosser makes it clear that these weapons have always posed more of a threat to the United States through the potentiality of accidents than to any U.S. adversary. It is hard to believe that the mathematicians, physicists, and engineers involved in nuclear weapons manufacturing were unable to complete the simple risk-reward analysis that would have brought into question the wisdom of building so many weapons, so it is not illogical to conclude that these missiles were built because once an economic structure was created around the building of missiles, it became almost impossible to *stop* building them.

Currently, just maintaining the nuclear force that the United States controls costs about $60 billion per year (https://www.cbo.gov/publication/57240#:~:text=If%20carried%20out%2C%20the%20plans,billion%20a%20year%2C%20CBO%20estimates) and the Apollo program cost close to $500 billion when adjusted for inflation, which is 45 times higher than the entire education budget for the state of Ohio in the 2021 fiscal year. These numbers are included because the actual cost of building the entire cold-war nuclear arsenal becomes too difficult to assess when one considers the vast supply chain expenses that would have gone into the whole program. Nonetheless, one could consider much of the American economy's mid-20th-century growth to have much in common with China's early 21st-century growth.

In 20th-century America and 21st-century China, massive make-work jobs created worthless objects. In the case of the United States, the Apollo rockets and 29,800 more nuclear weapons than were necessary were the product. In China, entire cities filled with apartments and work-buildings where no one has ever actually lived or worked are the product. In both cases, present debt was incurred for the purpose of increasing the gross domestic product.

It raises the interesting question posed by Graeber: how can an economic structure designed around the idea that money is paid for labor continues when automation means that less labor is actually needed? The current answer seems to be in the make-work response, where white-collar employees are required to show up for "work" regardless of whether there is anything much to do. Graeber makes two points about this: (1) Employers cannot seem to come to terms with the idea that they could just pay employees to be available when there is work. (2) If the government provided everyone with a basic living wage, regardless of whether anyone worked or not, then people would still work but employers would have to behave better because employees could quit when conditions became poor.

The second point might have seemed like fanciful speculation, except for the fact that the Great Resignation of 2021 and 2022 seems to confirm his thesis. If we could think of "Retirement" as a sustainable wage provided by an employer and/or the government, then it appears that millions of people retire and then continue to work in part-time forms of employment. The Great Resignation, where over four million people left the workforce in 2021, seems to have consisted largely of already-retired older people who gave up their part-time jobs in order to enter into full retirement (https://www.forbes.com/sites/avivahwittenbergcox/2021/11/16/the-great-resignationactually-a-mass-retirement/).

This would indicate that Graeber was right on two points. People will continue to work even if they have a guaranteed income, and they will also quit their jobs if the working conditions become too onerous. A guaranteed income would have the effect of creating a worker's market in virtually all fields and would force employers to be more flexible and humane in dealing with employees. These seem to be trends that are occurring in early 2022 as Google and other tech-sector employers are allowing their workers to eschew the office on a regular basis in favor of working from home. Freedom from the hierarchy has become a selling point for workers in the labor market.

The modern educational structure is needlessly stressful in some ways because the modern workplace is as well. A labor-for-money economy has turned into a subservience-for-money economy where white-collar workers suffer through seat-time jobs just to provide their bosses with someone to manage. This kind of a structure cannot be explained through rational economics, as billionaire celebrity CEOs like Elon Musk and Jeff Bezos hardly need any more money; they could each spend a life on perpetual vacation, as could almost all of the multimillionaires who enter into public office;

the power dynamic itself is what is purchased with the money; enough wealth allows for a CEO to create a social structure that he is dominant in; and that dominance can only be expressed if there are underlings.

In an earlier chapter, the effect that the perception of school quality has on property values, and the eventual effect that had on creating the housing bubble of the early 2000s, was explored. The economic effects of the housing meltdown, where the financial institutions that were supposed to be largely self-regulating on the premise that bankers and financiers employ a small amount of ethical reasoning, have been popularly understood as the kind of systemic fraud that no one was in charge of (and therefore not held accountable for) but that everyone in the system seemed to benefit from. In short, the narrative of the housing crisis goes like this:

Housing lenders began issuing "subprime" loans to borrowers who could not likely pay back their long-term loans. Those loans had built-in penalties for late payments, that made it impossible for borrowers who could not pay their mortgage payments to begin with. This allowed banks to push up profits based on a preconceived notion that mortgage lending was as stable as it had historically always been. As time went by, and more of the borrowers were forced to default on payments, those bad loans all came due at the same time.

Banks pay for insurance companies who are supposed to cover the cost of defaulted loans, but insurance companies work on the premise a defaulted loan will be a rare event. By analogy, an insurance company that insured 100 people against cancer treatment, would be "betting" that the number of people who will get cancer, at any one time, out of that 100 will probably be only 3 or 4. If something occurs where 50 of those 100 people develop cancer at the same time, the insurance company cannot make the payments and will have to declare bankruptcy.

In the case of the 2008 housing crisis, the sudden default of millions of loans overwhelmed the mathematical structure of the insurance companies. This meant that the banks and lenders would have to collapse, and since those lenders were "too big to fail" a massive government payout was issued with taxpayer money. A recession and then a recovery have slowly ensued.

That's the pleasant illusion, anyway. The reality is that the full financial crisis because the actual default chain has gone like this: Borrowers defaulted to the lenders, then the lenders defaulted to the insurance companies, then the insurance companies defaulted to the government, then the government defaulted to the national debt. The national debt is always a handy place to put a default because the cost gets rung up as a future expense.

The national debt is an interesting thing because the debt seems to cause no serious problems as long as regular payments can be made on it. However, with live births in the United States at an all-time low, and with no Baby Boom II in sight, eventually the number of taxpayers is going to shrink and the government's ability to make those regular payments will be compromised.

Here is where it gets interesting, and disturbing. According to the Wall Street Journal, older Americans in the United States are holding on to a collective $35 trillion (https://www.wsj.com/articles/older-americans-35-trillion-wealth-giving-away-heirs-philanthropy-11625234216). The post-WWII expansion of the American economy, coupled with entitlement benefits and longer lifespans, have created an economy that no one understands. The reason that no one understands this economy is because it is impossible to track the downward trickle of funds, from parents to their children or grandchildren, that is actually occurring in tens of millions of American households.

It is entirely possible, for example, that the American public education system only exists because young college students who want to be teachers are privately bankrolled in that enterprise by their parents and grandparents, a factor which might be also responsible for the well-known and much-lamented lack of diversity among K–12 educators. This might also be a factor in the egregiously high turnover rate that occurs among teachers, as some educators can leave teaching for other jobs because of accumulated family wealth. Again, this is not something that can be tracked, but $35 trillion is a lot of money and if even a fraction of that is being trickled down into families to help with education and to supplement low wages, then the economy is built on principles that no one fully comprehends.

How much of that $35 trillion will be siphoned off into late-in-life care for boomers? How much will be transferred to the government through inheritance taxes and how much will be transferred to the children and grandchildren of the deceased? Economists should be asking these questions, because if a significant chunk of that money gets handed down via inheritance, then there is the potential that a vast class of people in the country will not have to work at all, and will be holding on to "unearned" assets that might further exacerbate an economy where young people find themselves subservient to their parents and grandparents because they need access to wealth. In many ways, young people who go to college are finding themselves in perpetual servitude to their family elders, therefore unable to enter into independent adulthood, and working in jobs that seem to have no clear purpose.

The most cynical, and probably most accurate, way to view the American educational system's connection with the economy is as follows.

Hyper-competitive K–12 institutions are based on the idea that schools should both educate students and then winnow them into post-secondary education. The concept of equal access to education is not a serious one, it just provides the ideological precept that is necessary so that the system can declare that those who pass through the winnowing phase are deserving based on merit. From there, students who make it through the "meritocracy" are selected to either enter into elite post-secondary institutions or state colleges and universities.

The elite institutions prepare students to enter into a world of finance, where money is made from money and not from labor, or they enter into a legal or medical structure which is designed to both profit from and sustain the financial system. An Ivy League graduate can hardly waste such a prestigious education by being a teacher or a primary care physician, and so they slide into private-sector elite positions, working for banks, firms, and hospitals.

This class produces much value, in that pediatric neurosurgeons and professors who produce knowledge are derived largely from this group. However, these benefits must be countered by the fact that the two greatest American disasters of the 21st century, the American invasion of Iraq/Afghanistan and the 2008 housing crisis, were both almost entirely facilitated by Ivy League graduates who entered into politics and finance.

Commentators who lament that Americans have thrown their trust to know-nothing politicians might pause to think that the public might be rational in taking their trust away from the highly educated elites who, with perfect diction and reasonable demeanors, told them that the Iraq war was necessary for American national security, would be over in months, and would pay for itself. Those same elites kept up a concurrent lie about how low-wage workers could buy track housing with high-risk loans and do so without harming either themselves or the economy.

Those educated in lower-tier institutions can find jobs as teachers, nurses, accountants, engineers, and middle managers. Occasionally, individuals in these classes will overlap with individuals in the top tier, but for the most part these are useful jobs that have some type of beneficial effect on society. This class produces tangible benefits and the majority of taxable income for local and state governments. Somewhere within this class, however, are also those who graduate from college into the "bullshit jobs" discussed by Graeber.

While there is no such thing as unskilled labor, there is labor that is perceived to require less education. The word "perceived" in the previous sentence is key because hedge-fund management is not as complicated an intellectual enterprise as driving a 16-wheeler (which would you be more comfortable trying?); one assumes the complicated part of hedge-fund management is in finding the right connections to enter the field. Also, while it is probably never the case that truck drivers, plumbers, and HVAC workers ever actually need a financial analyst, it is almost always the case that financial analysts need them.

There would seem to be no point in describing the bottom of this social structure, where people are either materially or culturally impoverished. This is a world where an unintended pregnancy can derail an educational future, or where a DUI can prevent someone from entering into steady employment, or where a drug conviction or minor legal penalty that cannot be paid on a fixed income leads to a spiral of legal penalties and debt from which death provides the only escape. This class commits the types of crimes that the legal system is designed to deal with. White-collar criminals, like the perpetrators of the 2008 financial crisis or the higher education bureaucrats who have leveraged their credentialing abilities to the absolute hilt in order to take advantage of students with dreams, tend not to be imprisoned.

This hierarchical structure is propped up, ideologically, by the theory that education is the means by which someone can enter into the professions. Scholarships, student aids, and affirmative action are supposed to ensure the meritocracy. Any questions about why a young person would need to risk his brain playing football or soccer in order to gain a scholarship for the purpose of attaining an education get overwhelmed by cheers in the stadiums and by piles of money large enough to fill those stadiums.

Logic, therefore, leads us to a depressing conclusion: we are all working too hard for no good reason at all, and frequently to the detriment of ourselves. Take the examples above regarding both the NASA man-on-the-moon program (not to be conflated with NASA's general space exploration programs, which are worth the money for a variety of reasons) and the nuclear missile building binge of the Cold-War era. If the federal government had just paid all of those scientists, engineers, factory workers, and military personnel (who monitored, maintained, and practiced with the nuclear and space exploration rockets) to stay home and do nothing, what would be different?

The money from the government would have circulated into the hands of families, and the education they received in America's institutions would have provided access to the money, which is no different from an economic perspective than transferring the funds for work done. For the sake of discussion, it will be conceded that the United States likely needed about 500 nuclear weapons for national security purposes, but that means that 29,500 nuclear weapons were built that now need to be housed, maintained, and prevented from accidentally causing a catastrophe.

Had the government paid all those engineers, scientists, machinists, and soldiers to just stay home for most of the Cold War, then the economic growth would have looked the same, but we would not currently be faced with the menace of all of those corroding weapons. It might also be pointed out that the United States did not put a person on the moon between the years of 1776 and 1969, and has not done so since 1972. Neither the moon nor Earth seems to have suffered from such a lack of attention.

If we consider for a moment that the middle of the 20th century created an entire make-work industry in missile production, where engineers tried to move into management positions and where factory workers suffered from the malaise of repetitive industrial work, where soldiers endangered themselves (and everyone else!) by providing maintenance on the missiles and where universities created their engineering reputations by providing education for students who entered into those jobs. It is hard to think that the entire enterprise existed so that people could play make-believe that their work had meaning. However, to come to any other conclusion is to believe that the world would be better off with 29,500 corroding nuclear weapons that it would have been without them.

Also consider that the 2008 financial crisis cost Americans about $12.8 trillion, which equates to about $40,000 for every American. If the $12.8 trillion was just divided up and given to the 32.7 million Americans below the poverty line, that would have been the equivalent of $391,000, more than enough for those Americans to actually buy nice homes (https://finance.yahoo.com/blogs/daily-ticker/2008-financial-crisis-cost-americans-12-8-trillion-145432501.html?guccounter=1&guce_referrer=aHR0cHM6Ly93d3cuZ29vZ2xlLmNvbS8&guce_referrer_sig=AQAAAN178YnWIfeH0_B8n2ATS5Ue7PuxnL4Q08ZFf43wZ0M3Xr7maqoG1z9ami0h8q8Q5xxWt N9J6pdSxMxg3ZRWp-dUNgCRP1jnZ086VJtJ4r2a30OcwTDXTpGdVtXyr L1g5Bw-kAtQNumOuj6Hc8pxgsAPSTbRouKd9L0SloSuqDK3).

Before anyone tries to argue that just giving nearly $400,000 to poor Americans is bad policy because it causes inflation, etc., please consider that the alternative was to just give $12.8 trillion to a handful of banking firms who siphoned the money off to pay record bonuses to CEOs while almost immediately beginning to predate upon wishful loan-takers. The government, in effect, does just give that much money to the poor but they do so by needlessly distributing it through the banks who then make money off the money by taking interest payments. A direct investment of $400,000 apiece to anyone below the poverty line, for the purpose of home purchases, would have an immediate and broad stimulating effect across the economy because of the effect it would have on the housing sector and local businesses.

But this would be impossible to accomplish because of irrational components that remain a fundamental part of American politics and financial policies. America contains a core ideology that must be protected: that money is paid out for labor. This reluctance to pay money for not engaging in some kind of labor has generated a miserable make-work economy, and education seems to provide a means either into the middle of this economy where work can be meaningful, or to the top of it where work lacks almost all meaning. Meanwhile, actual work in the form of skilled trades and elder and child-care faces critical staffing shortages.

To change education is to change the workforce, if the modern workforce is filled with needless make-work jobs that are designed to enhance the prestige of the hierarchs. If there are not enough positions to provide meaningful work for educated people while blue-collar professions suffer from a lack of labor, then the educational process seems to mirror this messy and illogical system.

People are irrational when it comes to the sharing of resources. Again, if the lending sector can be viewed as the least effective means of distributing money to the poor, via high-interest sub-prime loans, then poverty could be largely eliminated and local economies improved if the government just gave about $400,000 apiece to anyone living below the poverty line. However, such an act would almost certainly infuriate taxpayers and those living close to the poverty line might be incentivized to drop their incomes. Local business people and building contractors might resent the fact that, although business would be flowing their way, they would have to work for money that other people had just been given.

And yet, in 2021, when COVID-19 vaccines became available, they were given out for free in Western societies without anyone seriously complaining that people should not just be handed something of value for no cost. Here was a vaccine of tremendous practical worth, but it was considered too important for society (and, one suspects, for the continuation of capitalism) to put a price on it. By analogy, society could just as easily consider general health care and a living wage to be as important for society as the COVID vaccine.

Then, in a phenomenon as interesting as it was/is disturbing, tens of millions of individuals who were eligible to receive the vaccine chose not to get it. These decisions were made despite abundant scientific evidence that the vaccinations were safe and highly effective. While a variety of underlying irrationalities can be blamed on the anti-vax movement, a public that is trained to see a free commodity as being a commodity without value, could not get over the suspicion that something about the vaccines served some purpose for those (choose your group, the government, big pharma, aliens) in power. Everything else operates under that principle, so why would vaccines be different?

Part of understanding a new vision for education is to understand that most forms of education and work are pleasurable in the right doses; this is why people read when they don't need a degree and work when they don't need the money. There is no reason why secondary education has to "winnow" students into competitive post-secondary schools and no reason why standardized tests need to operate as learning autopsies rather than as crucial components of a student's learning process.

We can all relax, the competition is killing us and making us less effective, and the entire process has no function but to maintain a hierarchical structure that is both illogical and stifles innovation. This last point deserves more commentary and will be elaborated upon in the next chapter concerning the connection between schools and the labor force.

Chapter 7

Workforce Development

Why does education seem so disconnected from the skills that are required in the workforce? This is not just an American problem; the much-discussed mathematics gap between American students and their East Asian counterparts seems to mean nothing at all in terms of quality of life. Students in South Korea, Singapore, and Japan who are pushed to develop their skills in mathematical hand-calculations, all of which can now be done with computer programs, might as well develop their talents in playing Scrabble, chess, or Go. These skills have almost no applications in the workforce anymore since computer-based algorithms control so much.

At one time, mathematics and science education was seen as being essential to the national defense industry but this is no longer the case. As of this writing, both North Korea and Iran, totalitarian backwaters where public education is almost nonexistent except for the purpose of indoctrination, are nearly capable of developing nuclear weapons. Pakistan, that dystopic caliphate, has possessed nuclear weapons for decades. Asian students might as well be learning how to hand-write out book manuscripts. American worries about the mathematics gap are arbitrary. Asian school administrators could just as well be worrying that American students, with their access to expensive athletic facilities, are far ahead of Asian students in the bench press and the squat.

Students everywhere spend hours studying subjects and worrying about tests that have no purpose at all anywhere in the workforce or in life. This disjunction leads some people to a state of near confusion. One of the most highly educated education public figures of recent years has been former South Bend Indiana mayor Pete Buttigieg, a Harvard/Oxford man and Rhodes scholar. While campaigning for the 2020 Democratic presidential nomination "Mayor Pete" would sometimes, apropos of nothing, start speaking in one of the six-to-eight languages he has supposedly mastered.

It was as if, having learned all of this, Buttigieg felt like it should be useful for *something*. One might imagine that, as president, Buttigieg's ability to speak six foreign languages would have come in handy should he have needed to meet with emissaries from any of those specific six nations. However, this brings up a question: is learning six languages so that, if one might become president then one could speak with emissaries from 6 of the world's 196 sovereign countries, a good use of time?

None of this is to say that learning languages, or how to hand calculate mathematical problems, is a bad thing. It is just to say that this form of learning should not be expensive because it will have no eventual payoff in the market. To reform education, and to preserve a place in society for subjects that may have no direct market value, a reconceiving of the purpose of education needs to be developed.

The point is that it should be possible to separate *lifestyle* (a better term than "lifelong") education from *workforce* education, and to understand that the two possess different types of meaning. Learning history, languages, mathematical hand calculations, and reading literature provide enjoyment and meaning. They may have residually positive effects on one's work life by either providing the learner with a sense of ethics or with thinking and comprehension skills that can be essential in seemingly unrelated situations.

But to tie a traditional classical or liberal arts education to the marketplace is inherently dishonest. Capitalism does not always reward ethical behavior or high levels of intelligence; one of the great fallacies of capitalism is that it assigns intelligence to a monetary level, and so individuals like Steve Jobs, Bill Gates, Elon Musk, or Jeff Bezos are assumed to be smart because they are rich. The contradiction here is that one can usually only become rich by creating products or services that the masses can use and understand, while high levels of intelligence are required at the edges of philosophy, science, or literature. Professional athletes are doing something that the public can understand, while philosophers and literary writers are just not. High intelligence rarely leads someone to personal riches.

There is also some evidence that the actual content of education might be less important for workforce innovation than attitude and culture. Top-down hierarchies, if too powerful, tend to prevent technological innovation. In his book, *Loonshots: Nurture the Crazy Ideas That Win Wars, Cure Disease, and Transform Industries* (2019), Safi Bahcall writes that "loonshots" are big ideas that appear counterintuitive and, therefore, may not receive the immediate structural support that they need. He writes:

> Drugs that save lives, like technologies that transform industries, often begin with lone inventors championing crazy ideas. But large groups of people are needed to translate those ideas into products that work. When teams with the

means to develop those ideas reject them ... those breakthroughs remain buried inside labs or trapped underneath the rubble of failed companies. (p. 7)

Later, Bahcall writes of something he calls the "Moses Trap" which he defines as:

> When ideas advance only at the pleasure of a holy leader—rather than the balanced exchange of ideas and feedback between soldiers in the field and creatives at the bench selecting loonshots on merit—that is exactly when teams and companies get trapped. The leader raises his staff and parts the seas to make way for the chosen loonshot. The dangerous virtuous cycle spins faster and faster: loonshot feeds franchise feeds bigger, faster, more. The all-powerful leader begins acting for love of loonshots rather than strength of strategy. And then the wheel turns one too many times. (p. 93)

In the rare cases where a new idea takes hold in a corporation and receives structural support, the producer of the idea can develop into a "Moses" (pick your famous CEO) and then innovation slows or stops because the culture of idea-sharing and cultivation becomes dependent on top-down decision making. The country of Israel provides an example of how a national environment that has cultivated the bottom-up challenging of authority, largely through their academic and military cultures, can channel those same types of attitudes into the culture of businesses.

In their book *Start-Up Nation: The Story of Israel's Economic Miracle* (2009), Dan Senor and Saul Singer wrote about Israel's impressive early 21st-century tech sector:

> Technology companies and global investors are beating a path to Israel and finding unique combinations of audacity, creativity, and drive everywhere they look. Which may explain why, in addition to boasting the highest density of start-ups in the world (a total of 3,850 start-ups, one for every 1,844 Israelis), more Israeli companies are listed on the NASDAQ exchange than all companies from the entire European continent.
>
> And it's not just the New York stock exchanges that have been drawn to Israel, but also the most critical and fungible measure of technological promise: venture capital.
>
> In 2008, per capita venture capital investments in Israel were 2.5 times greater than in the United States, more than 30 times greater than in Europe, 80 times greater than in China, and 350 times greater than in India. Comparing absolute numbers, Israel—a country of just 7.1 million people—attracted close to $2 billion in venture capital, as much as flowed to the United Kingdom's 61 million citizens or the 145 million people living in Germany and France combined. And Israel is the only country to experience a meaningful increase in venture capital from 2007 to 2008. (pp. 12–13)

Israel, a country with about the same geographic area as Delaware and the same population as Indiana, has turned itself into a global economic force that plays a major part in scientific advancement. This is all the more impressive given Israel's placement in a region that is usually noted for its political dysfunction, societal backwardness, and almost nonexistent infrastructure for scientific research. Outside of Israel, the only semi-functioning economies are those that, by geological lottery, have been allowed to evolve on top of massive oil reserves.

The authors credit Israel's economic success to the military training that is compulsory in the country. While traditional education is important in Israel, near-universal military service provides the Israelis with a particular kind of training that requires on-the-ground decision-making and the development of trusting relationships between commanders and subordinates.

Crucially, the Israeli Defense Force (IDF) operates with a largely decentralized structure. The authors quote an expert on the Israeli military, historian Edward Luttwak:

> . . . Luttwak began rattling off the ratios of officers to enlisted personnel in militaries around the world, ending with Israel, whose miliary pyramid is exceptionally narrow at the top. "The IDF is deliberately understaffed at senior levels. It means that there are few senior officers to issue commands," says Luttwak. "Fewer senior officials means more individual initiatives at the lower ranks."
>
> Luttwak points out that the Israel army has very few colonels and an abundance of lieutenants. The ratio of senior officers to combat troops in the U.S. Army is 1 to 5; in the IDF, it's 1 to 9. (p. 45)

Although Senor and Singer concede that such a format might not work as well with the much larger American military, the success of Israel's more egalitarian military structure can be measured in places far away from the battlefield. Soldiers who absorb such a culture in the military then carry with them the expectation that they will be treated equally and given decision-making capacity in their careers. This description states a lot about the IDF's culture:

> The dilution of hierarchy and rank, moreover, is not typical of other militaries. Historian and IDF reserve officer Michael Oren—now serving as Israel's ambassador to the United States—described a typical scene at an Israeli army base from when he was in a military liaison unit: "You would sit around with a bunch of Israeli generals, and we all wanted coffee. Whoever was closest to the coffee pot would go and make it. It didn't matter who—it was common for generals to be serving coffee to their soldiers or vice versa. There is no protocol about these things. But if you were with American captains and a major walked in, everyone would stiffen. And then a colonel would walk in and the major

would stiffen. It's extremely rigid and hierarchical in the U.S. Rank is very, very important. As they say in the American military, "You salute the rank, not the person." (p. 52)

The Israeli military was constructed from a bottom-up desire for existential survival, and with everyone so clearly believing in the mission, a kind of egalitarian start-up culture evolved and has been maintained. Soldiers and officers refer to each other by first names, soldiers routinely vote out their superior officers if they show incompetence. The stakes are too high for anyone to accept inferior decision-making. Israeli officers possess an authority that functions like tribal leaders in pre-contact Africa or the Americas did; they could only exert authority in so far as authorized by the people who entrusted them with the authority were willing to allow.

According to the authors, the Israeli military encourages soldiers to engage their officers with *chutzpah*, something that translates well into the business sector, where bosses sometimes need to be told they are wrong. Israel's decentralized military culture, where soldiers are empowered to make decisions on the ground according to the immediate need, and where superiors expect to be questioned, has created a highly effective business and political sector for the country.

Of course, it is impossible for Americans to use Israel as an example for workforce development because any discussion of Israel gets taken over by nonsensical arguments regarding the "occupation" of Palestine. Yet, in addition to their impressive work in the tech sector, Israel should be seen as a model of ethical restraint. The walls and fences partitioning Israel from Palestine evolved in response to one-way terrorist attacks. If Palestine, Iran, Egypt, or Lebanon were suddenly to possess the same kind of asymmetrical military power over Israel that Israel holds over them, then we would not likely see such a restrained approach. If, suddenly, *Hamas* held the military advantage over Israel, then it is unlikely that Israelis would merely find themselves on the opposite ends of fences and walls.

The example of Israel creates an interesting template; maybe young people need to be put into more situations where they have to think quickly, operate within a decentralized power structure, and learn how to allocate leadership based on talents and the quality of ideas rather than on hierarchical rank. In the United States, almost all forms of extracurriculars are arranged to give power to the adults.

Football coaches, especially at the high school and college level, are expected to act as authoritarians. Young men who march forward, brains crashing around inside their skulls, do so because they are ordered to. Band members who march their youth away in military formation do so because they are ordered to from (literally) above by a dictator standing on a platform.

Young people who engage in high school extracurriculars or athletics find themselves disempowered from decision-making, valuable to their coaches only insofar as their bodies help achieve meaningless victories.

Such an approach leads to an absurdity so common as to become unnoticed. Type "college and high school mascots" into a Google image search and you will be treated to images of snarling lions, angry tigers, fighting bears, ducks with their dukes up, triggered leprechauns, hyper-aggressive beavers, knights brandishing swords, eagles on steroids, a lot of Spartans and Trojans, chesty bulldogs, and more than a few devils. Mascots must stand for aggression, bluster, intimidation, and competition. To understand the mascot is to understand the ridiculousness of allowing competitive extracurricular activities to dominate education at the secondary and post-secondary levels.

One can imagine extracurricular and athletic activities that operate with on-the-spot decision-making and cooperation as the means to achieving a goal. It is also possible to think that the National Guard model could be adapted beyond the army. Programs like the National Guard put young people through basic training and the pay and benefits are not too bad given the limited time commitment. National Guard members very frequently find themselves filling in all sorts of emergency tasks, from providing support during natural disasters, to substitute teaching, to being shipped overseas to support military operations. A similar type of program could be created that might be separated from the military component, so that young people in the Guard might just be trained in a way that is more similar to firefighters or emergency medical responders.

In *Workforce Education: A New Roadmap* (2020) MIT professors William B. Bonvillian and Sanjay E. Sarma highlight several promising educational programs, short and focused, that prepare people directly for jobs. In their Introduction, they write about how states and the military are developing new types of certification and education programs. They write that ". . . short-term skill certificates, new immersive technologies, and tying community colleges more closely to employers with funding support—could even be combined" (p. 9).

Although these programs have yet to be fully vetted by research, workforce education that moves the students directly into open jobs would seem to have a meaningful future. *Workforce Education* is a comprehensive book that details the problems of trying to implement new programs in a disconnected, expensive, and bureaucratically hidebound education system, and the authors detail dozens of promising workforce programs that might be developed further in the future.

Sarma is also involved in the nascent blockchain credentialing movement which could allow students to develop their skills through online modules and carry with them a certification of their earned skill set. It is possible to foresee, for example, someone becoming a certified welder and also receiving a credential in mathematics, chemistry, or literature. Why would a welder choose to do this? One reason is that intellectual stimulation enhances one's life, another is that making educational opportunities cheap, or free, and allowing people to become educated while they are earning money and making a contribution to society might prove attractive.

There is also the potential that the government might recognize that it has a legitimate interest in seeing that working Americans are educated, say, in a basic understanding of mathematics, reasoning, and ethics so that those Americans might be able to examine false claims about vaccines, elections, school shootings, or Bigfoot sightings that can be found on social media or expounded by podcasting conspiracy theorists. Few people understand how to calculate probabilities, and will take "my cousin got the COVID vaccine and had a heart attack" anecdotes as more meaningful than a statement by the Centers for Disease Control and Prevention that the data shows no correlation between heart attacks and COVID vaccinations. People have heart attacks every day; if tens of millions of people get vaccinated, some people who were going to have a heart attack anyway will have them after receiving the vaccine. There is no more reason, however, to correlate the vaccination to the heart attack than there is to correlate the drive to the vaccination site to the heart attack.

Would a populace better educated in mathematics be less likely to take out sub-prime housing loans? Few people seem to understand that when one begins multiplying factors for a prediction, that the probabilities of something occurring get smaller. For example, if three people each have a set of shoes that are red, white, and blue the odds that those three people will show up at work in three red, three blue, or three white shoes are 1 (the odds that each will be wearing shoes to work, a near 100% probability) times .33 (the odds of any shoe choice) times .33 times .33. So the odds that the workers will show up with all red, all white, or all blue shoes are .035937, or about 3.6%. The odds that two in the group will be wearing red, white, or blue shoes are about 11%, and the odds that any individual will be wearing red, white, or blue shoes will be about 33%. The odds that everyone will be wearing shoes to work, barring some remarkable circumstance, are about 100%.

This is a simple statistics lesson, but an inability to understand how multiplying factors make something less likely rather than more and a misunderstanding of how probabilities break down into reality (when two people show up in white shoes, and one in blue, the odds of that happening were 3.6% but become 100% once it happens) cause confusion between predictions and reality. The opposite becomes true, for example, when individuals who are disinclined to believe in climate change see a cold snap in July as being refutation of a theory instead of watching large-scale trends in the temperature-collection data. How much more rational would life be if more people just understood the Law of Large Numbers?

All of this is to say that America's politicians might consider paying citizens to earn credentials in basic statistics, and what might loosely be termed "household" mathematics. And, while it might seem hard to understand why the government might be interested in having truck drivers read Toni Morrison, or learn the context of Shakespeare, one might ask the opposite question of "why not?" Is there any reason why the long monotony of highway driving could not be made intellectually profitable by people who could use that time to listen to lectures and audiobooks? If truck driving became an educational opportunity, then more young people might enter into a profitable profession that makes a contribution to society, and turn the truck cab into a mini-university. If a student wants to use those educational credentials to do something else later in life, so be it. If that student wants to continue driving a truck, then what's the harm in it?

If education has three functions, those being the development of a citizenry, the development of a workforce, and the cultivation of intellectual curiosity for the benefits of lifestyle learning there would seem to be no good reason to separate those functions from the MLM. They could all exist side-by-side and be accessed interchangeably by learners. If a student has access to the great benefits of face-to-face interaction with an instructor, then she should take advantage of that. If it's not available, for reasons involving geography or a busy time in someone's schedule, then an educational ecosystem can be accessed by anyone willing to be self-taught.

As of this writing, American K–12 education is under public pressure not seen since the days of segregation. The years 2021 and 2022 saw so many contentious school board meetings, many of which involved angry parents and community members essentially taking over the meetings after board members and administrators walked out, that Saturday Night Live spoofed the board meetings with a skit (an indicator that once mundane board meetings had entered into the public consciousness in a way that they never had before).

Community frustration with public schools began with the COVID lockdown, something which was originally ordered in 2020 by federal and state governments, but which continued in some areas based on decisions made by local school districts. For the first time since the Vietnam draft, parents and local communities emotionally felt the impact of governmental decisions on their lives. Unlike the draft, however, parents in communities where the schools were closed could focus their frustrations directly on a recognizable entity, the corporate school office, and the school board. Since board meetings are open to the public, school board meetings offered access to local officials and an outlet for frustrations that simply is not usually accessible to average Americans.

Conservative political operatives quickly found that they could channel that frustration into a movement against the inculcation of Critical Race Theory (CRT). A veteran teacher might be forgiven for seeing CRT as just more random fluff produced by the educational-methods salespeople. Variations on a "reversing racism" theme took place in untold numbers of school districts across the country. At first, the anti-racism training looked similar to the Ruby Payne "how to teach kids in poverty" craze that took place in the late 90s and early 2000s, or the Professional Learning Community concept that still infects schools and affects staff, but Payne was just peddling stereotypes about poverty and delivering a message that was comfortable for the white middle class (that message was that the purpose of schools is to teach impoverished students how to behave if they want to fit in with the middle class) while the reversing racism trainings brought the message that white people needed to reckon with the ongoing benefits that past and present forms of American racism have created.

The contradiction for anti-racists is (A) they make the case that American society is centrally defined by racism and that this needs to be corrected by reversing that process. Racism is not about individual behavior, but about systemic inequalities inherent in the structure that were created by racism and (B) that this circumstance could be fixed by convincing white people, through the educational structure, that this is true. The equivalent would be to give anti-religious training to young seminary students. If the anti-racist peddlers were correct in saying that American society was systemically racist to its core, did they really believe that such a society would respond to anti-racist trainings with an awakening, or did they expect a massive red-state backlash? Did it really matter to them as long as they made money?

Maybe the reason that Americans remain fixated on race is simple: it's the easiest thing to talk about. No body of knowledge needs to be mastered, no equations studied, no reading list exhausted in order to talk about race. One needs merely to walk around and have an experience in society; that experience becomes the basis of a conversation that, by definition, cannot be entered into by anyone who has a different race, sexual orientation, or gender identification from the person who initiates the conversation.

Such a concept is useful for a number of reasons as it becomes possible to dub any "difficult-to-understand" concept or equation as being a part of an inherently unequal structure. If the canon itself is arbitrary, then who decides that mastering arithmetic progressions or developing the ability to balance chemical equations is superior to mastering the experience of transgender people in society?

The Mastery-Learning Model provides a crucial dividing line. It's not possible to encode a social-engineering agenda into the MLM. There is no such thing as a body of knowledge based on individual experiences in society, unless one creates a curriculum around the literature of it. Even then, one would have to master the content and not the experience in order to pass a class. The MLM would simultaneously strip education of its social-engineering component and make such social-engineering unnecessary because a learner will be judged solely by the mastery of the content.

If and when that becomes the case, being the historical beneficiary of a racist/sexist society, or a beneficiary of the society's reengineering, will be of no use. Mastery of the content and skills will be all that matters and learners can carry their educational credentials through their lifetimes and into a variety of fields.

Conclusion
How Do We Do This?

As of this writing, public schools are, as is usually the case, a central feature of American controversy. Conversations about schools invite strong opinions, even political movements, regarding teachers' unions, vouchers, religion, and questions about whether the structure is inherently racist. None of these traditional arguments are relevant anymore. None of them help you, as the learner, to answer the essential question of "what would you do if you needed to learn something?"

Consider these questions:

A. Should states have school voucher systems?

   Vouchers don't teach anyone. They provide access to institutes of education that are seen as being "better" than the institute provided by the student's residential address. If MLMs are available, with the same education, in every school then what is the benefit of moving from one Seat-Time Model to another?

B. Do teachers' unions protect "bad" teachers?

   The MLM normalizes and standardizes the curriculum for every student. Teachers would be responsible for helping students through the MLM and would be treated as professionals who link the classroom with the surrounding community. Students would no longer be thrown into an education lottery where random assignments determine whether they get a highly effective teacher or not.

C. Are schools subject to systemic racism?

   If this is true, a student who wanted to learn trigonometry could completely circumvent a racist culture and just get a book of trig problems from the library and work through them with the aid of online modules.

A motivated student can now learn just about anything without needing to rely on such a structure.

The MLM will not take the place of public schools. The MLM will be implemented through public schools and will release the pressure put on teachers and students, especially the unsustainable amount of social and emotional pressures placed upon young people. Teachers will not cease to exist; they will just cease to be stressed-out and emotionally exhausted. They won't have to grade papers or tests, and more effective forms of professional development will allow them to connect with communities in higher education and the business/nonprofit world.

The medieval administrative class will no longer soak up so much of the taxpayer's wealth. Only a few administrators will be necessary.

Readers of this book will see that criticisms of MOOCs have been taken seriously and real solutions offered for the problems those criticisms address. In the anthology *What Should We Be Worried About: Real Scenarios That Keep Scientists Up at Night*, Daniel Everett contributed an essay titled "The Demise of the Scholar" that MOOCs are a threat because:

> Though MOOCs are unlikely to threaten elite universities, they will lead to many closings of smaller liberal arts colleges and branch campuses of state universities. Bill Gates predicts that a college education, through MOOCs, will soon cost only $2000 and that "place-based activity in that college thing will be five times less important than it is today. And with this loss of importance of colleges will come the demise of the teacher-scholar—the promoter of knowledge and scientific thinking. MOOCs will replace many universities, the employers of scholars, by online certificates." (p. 391)

Everett further worries about the loss of the informal sessions that students have over coffee and beer and states that "Replacing these experiences is not currently within the abilities or the objectives of MOOCs" (p. 392).

These are well-founded concerns and deserve to be answered. As Sanjay Sarma writes in *Grasp*: "Taking the broadest possible view, recovering vast quantities of latent learning potential—not to mention improving a whole lot of lives—is as simple as optimizing instruction while also improving access to it" (p. 230). A highly functioning MLM should not take anything away from an in-person experience. It could even be the case that a student who demonstrates a high level of mastery through an MLM could then gain access to institutes of higher education, a true meritocracy, where valuable face-to-face interactions occur between people who earned their way into the institution because they developed an interest in the subject and were disciplined enough to pursue mastery.

College campuses can be intimidating places, and not just because they tend to be arranged around a particular set of middle-class norms that people from inner-city or rural areas might find foreign. The layout of a class structure; the statement from the university that a particular set of courses must be taken, that students will spend the majority of their time in a subordinate position to an instructor, and that speech must conform to sometimes rigid behavioral boundaries all can constrict thought.

The great figures of the Scientific and Industrial Revolutions were almost entirely self-taught. In my book, *Femocracy: How Educators Can Teach Democratic Ideals and Feminism*, I noted that the great genius Mary Wollstonecraft likely benefitted from a lack of formal education. She learned from passionate private reading, and the culture of the book allowed her the freedom to dissent with the male philosophical figureheads (her inferiors), of Rousseau and Burke. Had she been a student of philosophy at a university, the environment almost certainly would have intimidated her away from her best thoughts.

Not to be hyperbolic, but the school structures can be compared to the colonial systems established by Europeans in the 18th and 19th centuries. Anticolonial works frequently spoke of how the structure of colonization elevated the Europeans to an undeserved status, but that it was beyond the capabilities of anyone to actually break out of the prescribed roles that colonization created. It was inevitable that the colonized populations would psychologically absorb a concept of inferiority; that's what hierarchical structures do to the people in them.

In the last several decades, a series of important thinkers have developed cross-disciplinary approaches to knowledge that go beyond the research model that has developed and sometimes inhibited the modern university. The STM is so inefficient that bureaucracies filled with mediocrities are required to keep the system running, always demanding more money and never making much of a contribution to the actual education of students. This medieval bureaucracy passes off absurdities, such as Howard Gardener's concept of "multiple learning styles" because that theory fits well with the customer service analogy that upholds the power of the administration.

Any thinking person who wants to see less radical type of educational reform should read anything by Ruby Payne, the poverty "expert" who has made a fortune off of professional development in schools, or the work of Rick and Rebecca Dufour, and explain how such a vapid set of ideas could proliferate so far in a professional environment. The fact that the work of Payne and the Dufours became so popular condemns the whole educational structure.

An MLM could be implemented across 13,600 school districts in the simplest of ways:

1. Bring together a small group of field experts and create Mastery-Learning Models. This might involve buying out existing models, such as MathandTutorDVD, which is impressive.
2. The Federal Department of Education would need to require, as a condition of receiving funds, that states offer that MLM beside the STM in public schools. This would include the new role for teachers and the new teacher professional development model described in this book.
3. Let students, teachers, and parents pick which model they want to engage with.

Those simple acts would shift the educational discussion in a meaningful way. Educational discussions for education must now, effectively, turn away from old arguments about charter schools, vouchers, and teachers' unions. It is now clear that the STM faces a serious challenge from the MLM. Which model prevails should be driven by the simplest question.

For me, that question is "what would I do if I needed to learn something?"

And the answer is "Read a lot. Write a lot. Consult tutorials when I have questions. Constantly take assessments. Seek out conversations. Take advantage of times when I can exercise or engage in daily necessities while visually or audibly consuming educational content."

When I need to learn something, I am in charge of that process. I am self-taught in that sense.

What would *you* do if you needed to learn something?

Ultimately, this will lead us to ask our students a different question. Instead of "what is it that you want to do?" We should ask them:

What contribution do you want to make?

Bibliography

Anderson, M. D. (2016). Students of color are disproportionately affected by school surveillance. *The Atlantic*. Atlantic Media Company. Retrieved September 12, 2016, from www.theatlantic.com/education/archive/2016/09/when-school-feels-like-prison/499556/

Arum, R., & Roksa, J. (2011). *Academically adrift: Limited learning on college campuses*. The University of Chicago Press.

Bernstein, W. J. (2021). *The delusions of crowds: Why people go mad in groups*. Grove Press.

Blase, J., & Blase, J. R. (2003). *Breaking the silence: Overcoming the problem of principal mistreatment of teachers*. Corwin Press.

Buttner, A. (2021). *The state of the teacher shortage in 2021*. Frontline Education. Retrieved July 4, 2021, from https://www.frontlineeducation.com/blog/teacher-shortage-2021/

Caplan, B. D. (2018). *The case against education: Why the education system is a waste of time and money*. Princeton University Press.

Carr, N. G. (2020). *The shallows: What the internet is doing to our brains*. W. W. Norton & Company.

Cbsnews.com. (2021). *Nearly 3 million U.S. women have dropped out of the labor force in the past year*. Retrieved July 4, 2021, from https://www.cbsnews.com/news/covid-crisis-3-million-women-labor-force

Chen, G. (2021). What is the connection between home values and school performance [Blog]. Retrieved April 26, 2021, from https://www.publicschoolreview.com/blog/what-is-the-connection-between-home-values-and-school-performance

Dave Campbell's Texas Football. (2021). *Sam Houston overcomes teammate injury to stun James Madison*. Retrieved July 4, 2021, from https://www.texasfootball.com/article/2021/05/08/sam-houston-overcomes-teammate-injury-to-stun-james-madison?ref=home_feature_article

Dehaene, S. (2021). *How we learn: Why brains learn better than any machine . . . for now*. Penguin Books.

Deresiewicz, W. (2015). *Excellent sheep: The miseducation of the American elite and the way to a meaningful life.* Free Press.

DuFour, R., DuFour, R., Eaker, R., & Karhanek, G. (2009). *Whatever it takes: How professional learning communities respond when kids don't learn.* Hawker Brownlow Education.

Flannery, M. E. (2018). The epidemic of anxiety among today's students. *NEA.* www.nea.org/advocating-for-change/new-from-nea/epidemic-anxiety-among-todays-students

Goldstein, D. (2015). *The teacher wars: A history of America's most embattled profession.* Anchor Books.

Guide2research.com. (2021). *101 American school statistics: 2020/2021 data, trends & predictions « Guide 2 Research.* Retrieved July 4, 2021, from https://www.guide2research.com/research/american-school-statistics#:~:text=In%20the%20U.S.%2C%20school%20districts,home%20to%2016%2C800%20school%20districts

Indystar.com. (2021). "It hurt so bad": Indiana teachers shot with plastic pellets during active shooter training. Retrieved July 4, 2021, from https://www.indystar.com/story/news/politics/2019/03/21/active-shooter-training-for-schools-teachers-shot-with-plastic-pellets/3231103002/

International Business Times. (2021). *UNC cheating scandal: Hundreds of fraternity brothers took "paper classes" to boost GPAs.* Retrieved July 4, 2021, from https://www.ibtimes.com/unc-cheating-scandal-hundreds-fraternity-brothers-took-paper-classes-boost-gpas-1711399

Korn, M., & Levitz, J. (2020). *Unacceptable: Privilege, deceit & the making of the college admissions scandal.* Portfolio.

Lieberman, D. (2021). *Exercised: Why something we never evolved to do is healthy and rewarding.* Vintage.

McCabe, D. L., & Bowers, W. J. (2009). The relationship between student cheating and college fraternity or sorority membership. *NASPA Journal, 46*(4), 573–586. 10.2202/1949-6605.5032

McDonald, D. (2017). *The golden passport: Harvard Business School, the limits of capitalism, and the moral failure of the MBA elite.* Harper Business.

Nash, L. K. (2005). *Elements of chemical thermodynamics.* Dover Publications.

Nextgov.com. (2021). *Remote work has two-thirds of Americans considering moving from cities to the country.* Retrieved July 4, 2021, from https://www.nextgov.com/cio-briefing/2020/10/remote-work-has-two-thirds-americans-considering-moving-cities-country/169598/

Osborne, D. (2017). *Reinventing America's schools: Creating a 21st-century education system.* Bloomsbury Publishing.

Pages.prompt.com. (2021). *Prompt—List of colleges that are accepting AP credits 2020.* Retrieved July 4, 2021, from https://pages.prompt.com/colleges-that-accept-2020-ap-credit#nochange

Pentland, A. (2014). *Social physics: How good ideas spread—the lessons from a new science.* Scribe Publications.

Sarma, S. (2021). *Grasp: The science transforming how we learn.* Anchor Books.

Strogatz, S. H. (2020). *Infinite powers: How calculus reveals the secrets of the universe.* Atlantic Books.

Thomsen, M. (2013). Get rid of grades. *Slate Magazine.* Retrieved May 1, 2013, from slate.com/human-interest/2013/05/the-case-against-grades-they-lower-self-esteem-discourage-creativity-and-reinforce-the-class-divide.html

Vlasova, H. (2021). *How many teachers are there in the US?—(facts & figures).* Admissonsly.com. Retrieved July 4, 2021, from https://admissionsly.com/how-many-teachers-are-there/#:~:text=Some%20teacher%20statistics%3A%20as%20of,million%20being%20in%20private%20schools

Westover, T. (2018). *Educated: A memoir.* Harper Collins Publishers.

Williams, A. E., & Janosik, S. M. (2007, November). An examination of academic dishonesty among sorority and nonsorority women. *Journal of College Student Development, 48*(6), 706–714.

www.nar.realtor. (2021). *Serve on a school board.* Retrieved July 4, 2021, from https://www.nar.realtor/articles/serve-on-a-school-board

"Zoom university": Is college worth the cost without the in-person experience? *The Guardian.* Guardian News and Media. October 6, 2020. www.theguardian.com/world/2020/oct/06/zoom-university-college-cost-students-in-person-experience

About the Author

Chris Edwards, Ed.D., teaches English and Advanced Placement World History at a public high school in central Indiana where he is also the ethics bowl coach. He is the author of numerous books with Rowman & Littlefield Education and Blue River Press. Chris is a frequent contributor to *Skeptic* magazine on the topics of law, logic, history, theoretical physics, psychology, and education. Chris has published and presented his original connect-the-dots teaching method with the National Council for Social Studies. As a facilitator and researcher, Chris created a summer STEM institute that focused on connecting secondary teachers with university STEM professors and with professionals in the STEM workforce. In 2018 and 2019, he became one of the only high school teachers to ever hold the position of principal investigator when he directed the Scientech/BSU summer institute program with state funding. Chris frequently speaks at science and educational conferences and was a guest on the Michael Shermer Show podcast.

www.ingramcontent.com/pod-product-compliance
Lightning Source LLC
Chambersburg PA
CBHW020126240426
43673CB00038B/609